Audio-Visual Anthropology

About the Author

Dr. M.S. Mahendrakumar is Assistant Professor in the Department of Anthropology, Kannur University in Kerala. He is the recipient of the first Ph.D. Degree (2004) of Kannur University, and the University was established in 1996. He is the Member of the Board of Studies in Anthropology (PG), and Member of the Faculty of Social Sciences, Kannur University. He was the Convenor of the First National Seminar on Visual Anthropology conducted by the Department of Anthropology, in collaboration with IGRMS, Bhopal and Anthropological Survey of India, Kolkata. He has worked in National and International Research Projects, and published a few research articles. He was also the Co-investigator of a two-year UGC Major Research Project (2005-2007). The book 'Pecuniarisation — A New Theory of Social Change in India' is his first book published in 2006. The theory of Pecuniarisation is one of his major contributions to the field of Socio-Cultural Anthropology. He has produced an ethnographic film in January 2010 entitled 'Indigenous People of a Wayanad Valley' (23 mts.). He was the Convenor of the Anthropology Film Fest 2010 conduced by the Department of Anthropology, Kannur University and Anthropological Survey of India, Mysore. 'Social Change Among the Cultivators' is his second book published in 2012. He is the Secretary of INCAA Kerala Chapter.

E-mail: ms_mahendrakumar@yahoo.co.in

AUDIO-VISUAL ANTHROPOLOGY

A New Version of Visual Anthropology

M.S. Mahendrakumar
Assistant Professor
Department of Anthropology
Kannur University, Thalassery Campus,
Palayad-670661, Kerala, India

CONCEPT PUBLISHING COMPANY PVT. LTD.
NEW DELHI-110059

ISBN-13 : 978-81-8069-921-4 (PB)

First Published 2013

Published and Printed by

Concept
Since 1974

Concept Publishing Company Pvt. Ltd.
A/15-16, Commercial Block, Mohan Garden
New Delhi-110059 (India)
T: 25351460, 25351794, *F*: 091-11-25357109
E: publishing@conceptpub.com, W: www.conceptpub.com
Editorial Office: H-13, Bali Nagar, New Delhi-110 015, India.

Cataloging in Publication Data--*Courtesy:* D.K. Agencies (P) Ltd. <docinfo@dkagencies.com>

Mahendrakumar, M. S.
Audio-visual anthropology : a new version of visual anthropology/ M.S. Mahendrakumar.
p. cm.
Includes bibliographical references (p.) and index.
ISBN 9788180699207 (hb.)
ISBN 9788180699207 (pbk.)

1. Anthropology—Audio-visual aids. 2. Visual anthropology. I. Title.

DDC 791.436552 23

Dedicated to my Father and Mother

M.V. Sukumaran & C.S. Saradambal

'Mayooram'
Cherussery
Thaikkattussery
Thrissur, Kerala

Preface

Visual Anthropology is a fast growing branch of anthropology with more emphasis on visuality of cultures. It emerged along with the development of photographic techniques. At present, Visual Anthropology has become a specialisation in anthropology. Though the ethnographic filmmakers are making films and mixing sound, at the conceptual level the use of sound has not been delineated as an important aspect, which virtually motivated me to think about the inevitability of audio along with visual and this outlook persuaded me to make a holistic framework for the study of audio and visual aspects of human culture. During several decades, the usefulness of photographs and film or video have attracted most of the people in the discipline of anthropology. Through this book, I have made an attempt to provide the history of development of visual anthropology succinctly; and moreover I am humbly placing 'Audio-Visual Anthropology' as a new version of Visual Anthropology in front of the anthropologists of the world.

The audio-visual behaviour of man has extreme significance in anthropology as it is through these two fundamental ways man communicate each other most of the time. The emphasis on audible element of human communication is more critical like the visuality of cultures. This point of view, of course, provides a rethinking on visual anthropology, which possesses strength to this new version, Audio-Visual Anthropology.

Recording original audio without noise and distortion while shooting outdoors and making an ethnographic film is a challenging task. However, the authenticity and originality can be maintained through various methods of filmmaking and sound recording. The original audio along with the real cultural situation of the people is extremely important. It is in this juncture, this book points out the shift of emphasis of Visual Anthropology to Audio-Visual Anthropology. This new version, nevertheless, does not discard any of the positive features of Visual Anthropology, but it is adding a new dimension to Visual Anthropology.

While developing this new perspective, I have published an article in 'Kerala Calling', a Government of Kerala publication, through which I have provided the definition for 'Audio-Visual Anthropology' for the first time in 1997.

In 2001, I have presented a paper entitled 'Relevance of Audio-Visual Anthropology and its Application' in a National Seminar held by the Department of Anthropology of the University of Mysore in Karnataka State, in India.

In 2005, I have presented another paper 'Concept of Visual Anthropology and Audio-Visual Anthropology' in the National Seminar on Visual Anthropology organised by the Department of Anthropology, Kannur University, Kerala, in collaboration with the Anthropological Survey of India, Kolkata and the Indira Gandhi Rashtriya Manav Sangrahalaya (IGRMS), Bhopal, in India.

In 2007, the paper entitled 'Audio-Visual Anthropology and Its Application: A Conceptualisation' has been published in the book review journal — 'Review Projector (India)', Tatabad, Coimbatore, Tamil Nadu.

In 2010, I have presented another paper entitled 'Audio-Visual Anthropology: A Conceptualisation' in the Third Indian Anthropological Congress, organised by Indian National

Confederation and Academy of Anthropologists (INCAA) at Indira Gandhi Rashtriya Manav Sangrahalaya (IGRMS), Bhopal.

In fact, I took much more time to formulate this new version and this is not a terminological shift but it is a conceptual, theoretical, and practical shift of 'Visual Anthropology' to 'Audio-Visual Anthropology'. This book is the outcome of an extensive study on the areas of Visual Anthropology, Visual Media, Audio-Visual Communication, Social and Cultural Anthropology and Linguistics.

'Audio-Visual Anthropology: A New Version of Visual Anthropology' is my third book. 'Pecuniarisation—A New Theory of Social Change in India' was my first book, published in 2006. 'Social Change among the Cultivators' is my second book published in 2012.

During the research days of my Ph.D. programme, I have used Video Camera and Still Camera throughout my fieldwork. During those days, I have recorded, nearly 16 hours, the lifestyle of the village people in video in 1996. Later on, it was edited with linear editing machines and finally it was edited with non-linear editing software. The experience which I gained from the various stages of video production, that is from research scripting to shooting, editing both linear and non-linear, sound recording and mixing, and all these paved the way for the preparation of this book.

Besides that, in January 2010, I have produced an anthropological video film entitled 'Indigenous People of a Wayanad Valley', which was telecasted in VICTERS, the educational television channel of the Government of Kerala. The duration of the film is 23 minutes and it gives a brief ethnographic account on the tribal people of Wayanad district in Kerala, namely, the Wayanad Kadars, Kattunaickans, Paniyas, and the Kurichians. The DVD of the film was released by Prof. (Dr.) A. K. Danda in the Third Indian Anthropological Congress held at the IGRMS, Bhopal on 21st February, 2010, and I am extremely grateful to

Prof. Danda and the Indian National Confederation and Academy of Anthropologists (INCAA), West Bengal.

Ample knowledge in anthropology and analytical mind are the two important requirements in formulating a new version of anthropology, for which I am extremely thankful to my anthropology teachers. At this moment, first of all, I am extremely grateful to Prof. (Dr.) B. Ananda Bhanu, the former Head (Retd.) of the Department of Anthropology, Kannur University, Kerala, who has been a fountain of wisdom in my anthropological endeavours.

Moreover, I would like to acknowledge my gratitude to a few scholars, friends, and relatives. I am extremely thankful to my friend Mr. T.J. James, Anthropologist, and Consultant in National Innovation Foundation Ahmedabad, and also Chevening Scholar, Said Business School, University of Oxford.

I am very grateful to Dr. M. Sasikumar, the former Director, KIRTADS, Calicut and presently the Deputy Director, Anthropological Survey of India, Andaman Islands, for the constructive suggestions.

Mr. C.A. Vijaya Raghavan, Selection Grade Lecturer (Retd.), Department of Sanskrit, Government College, Thrissur, has been a fountain of wisdom in my academic ventures and I am extremely grateful to him. I wish to convey thanks to Dr. C.P. Vinod, my friend and former colleague in the International School of Dravidian Linguistics, Thiruvananthapuram.

I would like to express extreme gratitude to Dr. K. Dinesan, Assistant Librarian (Retd.), and Mrs. Sujatha Aniyeri, Assistant Librarian, Campus Library, Kannur University, Thalassery Campus, Palayad. I also would like to express my sincere thanks to Mr. K. Balachandran, the former Librarian, International School of Dravidian Linguistics, Thiruvananthapuram.

I am thankful to my friends Dr. S. Bindu, Director, KIRTADS, Calicut, Mr. Hareendran P., Assistant Director, Dr. K.S. Pradeep Kumar, Research Officer, Mr. Subash V.S., Research

Officer, Ms. Mini P.V., Research Officer, and Mr. K.P. Suresh, Research Assistant, KIRTADS, Calicut, and all of them were helpful throughout my academic endeavours and I am acknowledging them here.

I am also grateful to my colleagues Prof. (Dr.) Vineetha Menon, Dr. S. Gregory, Dr. B. Bindu, and Dr. M. Sini, Department of Anthropology, Kannur University. The discussions with my colleagues and students have strengthened and streamlined my writings and therefore I am extending my heartfelt thanks to all the faculty members and students of the Department of Anthropology, Kannur University, Kerala, in India.

I have learned, during my childhood, the basics of shooting, editing, and sound dubbing in the 8 mm film format since an 8 mm movie camera and a film projector were there in my home, and my father taught me the basics of the camera operation, editing, etc., and I am extremely thankful to my father, M.V. Sukumaran, Drawing Teacher (Retd.) of the Nalanda High School, Kizhuppillikkara, in Thrissur district of Kerala. I have also learned the basics of drawing, oil painting, photography, music, and script writing from my father. My mother C.S. Saradambal, and my wife Sali, V.S. and my daughters M.M. Niveditha and M.M. Noopa have patiently co-operated with me while writing this book and I am extremely thankful to all of them. I am also thankful to Anjana V.M., Anoopkumar V.M., Jithin M.G., and Abhinav M.A., for their help and assistance.

Palayad
4-1-2012

Dr. M.S. Mahendrakumar
Assistant Professor
Department of Anthropology
Kannur University
Thalassery Campus
Palayad P.O., Kerala, India

Contents

1
Visual Anthropology

Visual anthropology is a fast growing branch of anthropology and it is emerged along with the development of photographic techniques. At present, visual anthropology has become one of the specialisations in anthropology. Many students and scholars across globe study visual anthropology. Some universities are providing M.A. or M.Sc. courses in Visual Anthropology whereas some are providing it as an Elective Paper and some universities provide P.G. Diploma in Visual Anthropology. In general, the growth of this sub-discipline is tremendous today.

Anthropologists are utilising the constructive features of photography to document the visuality of human cultures and social behaviours in Still Photos and Motion Pictures. In ethnographic studies, photographs provide additional strength and credibility to the rhetoric descriptions on cultures and societies. Instead of the descriptive accounts of ethnography, the makings of visual documents on cultures have attained extreme importance as it can preserve the actual life situations in films or digital visual documents.

The dynamic nature of cultural organisation, disorganisation, and reorganisation of mankind has been a concern of anthropologists since the inception of the subject anthropology. E.B. Tylor (1871), the "Father of social anthropology", has mentioned on the survivals of cultures in the form of proverbs, which remains today despite the actual practices have vanished from various societies. The existence of distinguishing features of a society on the one hand and the vanishing of cultural traits or practices on the other hand have virtually tempted to adopt the photographic techniques to encode such human activities for further research and analysis, which paved the way for the development of visual anthropology.

Anthropology is an eclectic discipline, which has been developed with the critical thinking of scholars from various disciplines including biology, medicine, geography, physics, etc., and similarly anthropology has been adopted and developed different methods for the study and analysis of human biological and social aspects. In the case of visual anthropology, the anthropologists and filmmakers have worked together to develop this branch and most of the techniques and methods of filmmaking are inevitable for visual anthropology.

Visual Anthropology: Concepts and Scope

The term 'Visual Anthropology' was coined by Margaret Mead in the 1960s. Mead (1975 : 10) is of the opinion that "camera gives the verbally inarticulate medium of expression and can dramatize contemporaneously an exotic culture for its own members and for the world, as anthropologists we must insist on prosaic, controlled, systematic filming and videotaping, which will provide us with material that can be repeatedly reanalysed with finer tools and developing theories."

There are a number of definitions for visual anthropology. Sahay (1993 : 3), an Indian anthropologist, is of the opinion that "visual anthropology is inextricably connected with photography, whether it be still photographs or films on the life and culture of various people that are used for teaching, research, feedback, or other applied purposes." Sahay further stated that, "Visual anthropology is generally understood as studying man and his culture by employing camera as its principal instrument of investigation that may produce either still photographs or moving images to be seen on a screen" (*ibid.* : 35). In these definitions, it is emphasised on the importance of the use of camera for cultural documentation.

In the words of Roy and Jhala (1992 : 16) "there is no consensus on a single definition, broadly speaking visual anthropology is the study of mankind, employing as its principle instrument of investigation the camera."

Ruby (1996 : 134) says "in practice visual anthropology is dominated primarily by an interest in pictorial media as a means of communicating anthropological knowledge, that is, ethnographic films and photographs and, secondarily, the study of pictorial manifestations of culture."

Among the various concepts on visual anthropology, the general as well as most important aspect is the use of camera for making visual images of cultures. Scupin (1995 : 120) has rightly cautioned that "ethnologist must use extreme caution when using tape recorders [audio recorders] and photography for in some cultures people are very sensitive about being recorded or photographed. Another problem mentioned is that there is one drawback to video recording is that people who know they are being filmed frequently behave differently from the way they would normally. This may distort the ethnologist's conclusions."

This is a turning point in the practice of visual anthropology because conceptualising is comparatively a trouble-free aspect whereas doing something or materialising a task without much trouble is a complex thing in visual anthropology.

History and Development of Visual Anthropology

The history and development of visual anthropology is directly related to the history of the development of ethnographic films. In the formulation of the subject visual anthropology, the

International Conference on Visual Anthropology held in Chicago in 1973 at the University of Illinois as a part of the IXth International Congress of Anthropological and Ethnological Sciences have played a great role. The publication of those 32 papers in the volume 'Principles of Visual Anthropology' edited by Paul Hockings is a landmark in the development of visual anthropology. The titles of papers are as follows:

'Visual Anthropology in a Discipline of Words' by Margaret Mead, 'The History of Ethnographic Film' by Emilie de Brigard, 'McCarty's Law and How to Break It' by Mark McCarty, 'Cinematic Social Inquiry' by Gerald Temaner and Gordon Quinn, 'Observational Cinema' by Colin Young, 'The Camera and Man' by Jean Rouch, 'Documenting the Human Condition' by Jorge Preloran, 'Beyond Observational Cinema' by David Mac Dougall, 'Ethnographic Film Documents' by Roger Sandall, 'Idea and Event in Urban Film' by John Marshall and Emilie de Brigard, 'Ethnographic Observation and the Super-8 Millimetre Camera' by Richard Leacock, 'Research Filming of Naturally Occurring Phenomena: Basic Strategies' by E. Richard Sorenson and Allison Jablonko, 'Ethnographic Film and History' by Jean-Dominique Lajoux, 'Some Methods of Ethnographic Filming' by Alexei Y. Peterson, 'Reconstructing Cultures on Film' by Asen Balikei, 'The Role of Film in Archaeology' by Stuart Struever, 'Photography and Visual Anthropology' by John Collier, Jr., 'Feature Films as Cultural Documents' by John H. Weakland, 'Videotape: New Techniques of Observation and Analysis in Anthropology' by Joseph H. Schaeffer, 'The Film Elicitation Technique' by Stephanine Krebs, 'Audio-visual Tools for the Analysis of Culture Style' by Alan Lomax, 'Filming Body Behaviour' by J.H. Prost, 'A Photographic Method for the Recording and Evaluation of Cross-Cultural Proxemic Interaction Patterns' by Shawn E. Scherer, 'Proxemic Research: A Check on the Validity of Its Techniques' by Robert

F. Forston, 'Educational Uses of Videotape' by Paul Hockings, 'Using Film in Teaching Anthropology: One Pedagogical Approach' by Timothy Asch, 'The Use of Television in Teaching Anthropology' by Jamshed Mavalwala, 'Research Films and the Communications Revolution' by Foster O. Chanock and E. Richard Sorenson, 'Mass Communication Meets the Anthropologists: A Short Manual of Some Unprimitive Thought' by Jay K. Hoffman, 'Anthropological Programming in Japanese Television' by Junichi Ushiyama, 'The Tribal Terror of Self-Awareness' by Edmund Carpenter, and 'Visual Records: Human Knowledge and the Future' by E. Richard Sorenson. The compilation of fragmented thoughts on visual anthropology was accomplished by the International Conference.

In India, according to Singh (1992) "many streams have contributed to the development of what we call visual anthropology in India. The colonial ethnographers, the film and documentary makers, freelancers, anthropologists and the AnSI [Anthropological Survey of India] in the post-colonial phase, and various other organisations including the university departments of anthropology and autonomous scientific organisations have been active in this area." In India, the first International Seminar on Visual Anthropology was held in Jodhpur in 1987. The proceedings of the seminar was published in 1992, entitled 'Visual Anthropology and India', which consists of 13 papers, namely, 'Cultural Policy, Cultural Pluralism and Visual Anthropology: An Indian Perspective' by K.S. Singh, 'An Examination of the Need and Potential for Visual Anthropology in the Indian Social Context' by Rakhi Roy and Jayasinhi Jhala, 'TV Portrayal in India: Some Observations' by J.S. Yadav, 'An Intelligent Critic's Guide to Indian Cinema' by Ashis Nandy, 'Rethinking the Subject of Ethno-documentary' by Trinh T. Minh-ha, 'Ethnographic Film and the Instrumentalist Approach' by Roger Sandall, 'Some Ethical Considerations Applied to Ethnographic Filmmaking: A Personal View' by Timothy Asch,

'Filming in the Field of Anthropology' by John Marshall, 'A Cameraman's Perspective on Visual Anthropology' by Richard Leacock, 'The Production of Cultural Pluralism as a Process' by Sally Falk Moore, 'Margaret Mead Film Festival: The First Decade' by Malcolm Arth, 'Ethics of Preservation Versus Ethics of Presentation' by P. K. Nair, and 'The Commission on Visual Anthropology, IUAES—Some Recent Activities' by Asen Balikei.

Today, the impact of Visual Anthropology has reached to all the people across the globe. In Kerala, a southernmost State in India, the first National Seminar on Visual Anthropology was held in 2005 and the Department of Anthropology, Kannur University, in Kerala, organised the Two Day National Seminar on Visual Anthropology in collaboration with the Anthropological Survey of India, Kolkata, and Indira Gandhi Rashtriya Manav Sangrahalaya, Bhopal. The titles of the papers are as follows: 'Ethnographic Films and Tribal Affairs: The Todas of Nilgiri Hills, Tamil Nadu' by Jakka Parthasarathy, 'Concept of Visual Anthropology and Audio-Visual Anthropology' by M.S. Mahendrakumar, 'Pilgrim Centres along the Kaveri River in Karnataka and Tamil Nadu: A Visual Presentation of Sacred Geography and Sacred Performances' by H.K. Bhat and S. Mahadeva, 'Rehabilitation and Resettlement Programmes for the Tribes Distributed in the National Parks' by H.M. Maralusiddiah Patel and H.M. Ganesh, 'The Kodavas of Karnataka: People and their Culture' by Rajasekhara Reddy and Subramanya C.E., 'The Death Ritual among the Jenu Kuruba' by B.R. Vijayendra, 'Life Cycle Rituals among the Adi-Karnataka People in a Mysore Village' by Veena R., 'Social Life of the Rehabilitated Jenu Kurumbas of Nagapura—A Visual Presentation' by Suresh B. Ramachandraiah, 'Rituals of the Gowda Saraswath Brahmins and the Pitarar' by Sona E., 'Visual Art in Indian History' by Varun Thampan and Anushree B., 'Relevance of Audio-Visual Repertoire' by K. Dinesan and

Muhammed Najeeb V., 'Modern Technologies and Media Culture' by S. Josh, 'Pottery Tradition among the Anthur Nairs of Kerala' by Sini M., 'The Primitive Tribal Groups of Kerala: A Situational Appraisal' by Seetha Kakkoth, 'Glimpses of Tribal Archery in Kerala' by Mini, P.V., 'Spatial Organisation of a Matrilineal Taravad—A Case Study' by B. Bindu, 'Symbolic Aspects of Culture among the Malavedan Tribes of Kerala' by Pradeep Kumar K.S., 'A Ritual Art in Transition: A Case Study of Gadhika of the Adiyans of Wayanad' by Subash V.S., 'Theyyam—A Ritual Dance of North Kerala' by Rimina Raghavan and Suthipta, and 'An Anthropological Study on Melkote and Keretonnur Villages in Mandya District, Karnataka: A Visual Presentation' by C.K. Kantharaju and H.K. Bhat. The papers presented in the Two-Day National Seminar on Visual Anthropology have virtually stimulated the interests of scholars in visual anthropology.

The above Chicago Conference and Jodhpur Seminar discussed various conceptual and theoretical aspects whereas the Kerala Seminar portrayed the case studies of various populations, which shows the growth of the discipline and the application side as well as the acceptance of the discipline among the students and scholars of anthropology in India.

2
Ethnography and Ethnographic Films

"We can cherish those rare combinations of artistic ability and scientific fidelity that have given us great ethnographic films." (Margaret Mead, 1975 : 5)

Ethnography

The term 'ethnography' has to be defined prior to the discussions on ethnographic films. According to a common understanding, ethnography means the scientific description of the races of the earth, whereas ethnology means the science that treats the varieties of human race; and cultural anthropology is also used as a synonym for ethnology.

Tylor (1871) defined ethnography as the study of individual cultures. It is primarily a descriptive and non-interpretative study. The term 'ethnic' also has been defined as it referring to a group distinguished by common cultural characteristics. Further, he conceptualised 'ethnology' as the study of culture on a comparative basis and the theory of culture; it is often called cultural anthropology. Ethnology is distinguished from ethnography as being more inclined towards theory and the comparative study of institutions. It was widely used as a synonym for anthropology. The term is also found in some European usages as meaning ethnography.

New Ethnography

New ethnography is referred to as autobiographies or autoethnographies. It is also considered as creative narratives of a culture. Ethnography is the study of individual cultures. Comparative study of cultures is known as ethnology. New ethnography is emphasising on the creativity of writing cultures.

History of Ethnographic Filming

According to Brigard (1975 : 15), Felix-Louis Regnault was the first person to make an ethnographic film. Regnault filmed a Wolof woman making pots in 1895 and the film showed the Wolof method of making pottery, using a shallow concave base which is turned with one hand while the clay is shaped with the other. Regnault published his article on the very experiment in December 1895, which was the month and year of the first successful public projection of a commercial cinema that triggered the motion picture industry. In 1898, Alfred Cort Haddon used a Lumiere camera to make an ethnographic film during the Torres Straits Expedition (Brigard, *ibid.*).

Torres Straits Expedition "...was an expedition to the Torres Straits in 1898 led by A.C. Haddon and including C.S. Myers, C.G. Seligman, W.H.R. Rivers, and A. Wilken. It was the first anthropological field trip in which the interdisciplinary team approach was used. Rivers' paper, *A Genealogical Method of Collecting Social and Vital Statistics* and Myers' work on the psychology of sense organs resulted from the expedition, which also set high standards for future fieldwork and publication" (Tylor, 1988 : 198).

According to David Mac Dougal (1976), Flaherty's *Nanook of the North* is considered to be the first ethnographic film and that black and white film was released in 1922, which was based on the life and culture of the Eskimos of the North Pole. Robert Flaherty,

David Mac Dougal with a 16 mm movie camera

a Canadian explorer turned cinematographer documented the story of an Eskimo family and its fight for food. One text frame of the film provides "This picture concerns the life of one Nanook (The Bear), his family and little band of followers, 'Itivimuits' of Hopewell Sound, Northern Ungava, through whose kindliness, faithfulness and patience this film was made" (from one text frame of the film *Nanook of the North*). In the words of Mike Wolverton (1987 : 8) "*Nanook* was a whole new kind of film, never heard of before by the producers of slick formula stories of melodramatic impact... As a true document of everyday life with selectivity of detail and sequence, and intimate camera work, its dramatic value impressed the Hollywood producers tremendously." Flaherty used text frames and visual frames, one after the other, to communicate the film most effectively.

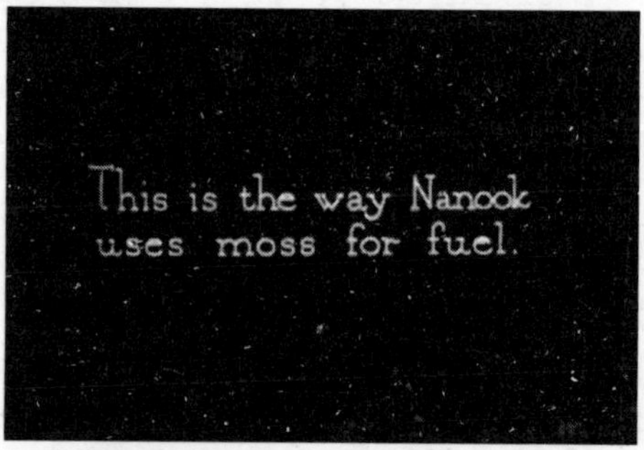

Text Frames"From the Nanook of the North

Movie frames"from the Nanook of the North

But, according to Peter Harris-Jones (1998 : 64), "Gregory Bateson is best remembered among anthropologists for producing one of the first ethnographic films, which he made together with his wife, Margaret Mead, in Bali between 1936 and 1938."

John Marshall and Robert Gardiner together produced the film 'The Hunters' in 1956. At present, a large number of filmmakers and scholars all-over the world are making a lot of ethnographic films.

Ethnographic Film

Ethnographic film is an outcome of the blend of anthropology and filmmaking. Filmmaking is underscoring the relevance of photography. And filmmaking is based on the visuals and sound. The effective use of the audio-visual media in providing an anthropological depiction is more important. This would normally end with a product, which will be an admixture of anthropology and filmmaking; and it is generally referred to as ethnographic film or anthropological film.

Films can reproduce the objects of our world photographically and the value of photography as a supplement to written records became unquestioned. At the same time, some of the film theoreticians like Arnhaim, observed the possibilities of this medium in depicting the real life and he has written it in 1950s. According to him, "the technical development of the motion picture will soon carry the mechanical imitation of nature to an extreme. The addition of sound was the first obvious step in this direction". That is the addition or use of sound to the photography inverted the emphasis from picture (photography) to a word to word (nothing but sound) to a picture. This novelty of the medium attracted the pioneers of ethnographic filmmaking and accordingly they, for instance, Flaherty, John Marshall, Robert Gardiner and others have attempted to depict man's culture in films or audio-visual media.

Ethnographic filming fixed its roots in anthropology, among anthropologists and some filmmakers throughout the world. It has been a major area of interest of visual anthropology. Ruby (1996 : 1346) has rightly pointed out that "ethnographic film is the dominant interest and practice among visual anthropologists."

Bock says, "if one picture were really worth thousand words, most ethnographic reports could be shortened to perhaps fifteen pages of plates" (1969 : 394). It is unquestioned or it is widely accepted that the pictures are very valuable and supplementing obvious information to written records. Bock (*ibid.*) further cautions that "photography ... its value as a supplement to written records is unquestioned, but it must be remembered that the camera is selective as well as objective, so that the taking and interpretation of photographs is a difficult affair. In recent years, there has been increasing interest in the potentialities of ethnographic films, but these are both difficult and expensive to make. Like life histories and psychological tests, motion pictures can be meaningful only when the fundamental cultural patterns of social group are fully understood and good rapport has been established. An ethnographic film made for teaching or aesthetic purposes will be very different from one intended solely as a record of observations. Good films of any of these types are still extremely rare. The most successful of these films have been the result of intimate collaboration between an experienced ethnographer and an imaginative professional filmmaker."

Ethnographic film has been hesitant in its pursuit of the other, hesitant in reference to the very innovations and their developments. The ethnographic film tradition of operation follows four parallel streams such as:

1. Documents innovations in production technology,
2. Innovations in evolving and shifting treatment of the subject matter of this genre of films,
3. Innovations in the strategies of argument brought to the film and television viewer, and
4. Questions that speak to the issue of ethnographic authentication.

Mead has emphasised the need of training for ethnographers in ethnographic filming as she "believes the best work [ethnographic film] is done when filmmaker and ethnographer are combined in the same person, although in many cases one interest and skill may outweigh the other" (Mead, 1975 : 7).

The Relevance of Ethnographic Films

The relevance of ethnographic film is quite significant today, and it calls our attention to the life of contemporary man and its backdrop—the society. Society is sustaining its nature of replacing culture traits. At all time society has showed its own agreements and disagreements on culture, and it has been attracting many anthropologists and social scientists. But, with the advent of modern developments many traditional societies have got acculturated. Then, with the technological developments there have had great many changes and it in turn changed the culture of man and his technology. The technological development is pervasive and it has been touched on photographic and filmmaking technology too, and the very development laid the foundations of "art of filmmaking".

Rightly, in anthropology there is no place for shouting to preserve traditions in such entities, in order to exhibit the contemporary culture forever, because the very culture change is happening from the time immemorial.

Of course, the nature and extent of dynamics in inter-human and non-human relations have not always and everywhere been uniform. Today, the pace of change in societies, however, seem to be a little abrupt than the past and there is a growing tendency and interest have developed all-over the world to make ethnographic films in order to preserve the age-old practices or cultures at least in videos, films, CD, DVD, Blue-Ray Disc, etc.

Digital Ethnography

It is a way of capturing ethnographic data in a highly preservative manner by using digital cameras. Digital ethnography is a term evolved with the introduction of digital photography and digitalization of visual data. Analogue technology was replaced by the digital technology and with the introduction of digital technology, filmmaking and sound recording have become more simplified, and more flexibility is there in the digital technology. At present, ethnographers are using digital video cameras to make ethnographic films, which are referred to as Digital Ethnography.

Visual Ethnography

Visual ethnography is a visual account of an ethnographic study.

Instead of textual descriptions, anthropologists use film/video camera to study the cultures of various societies. Both anthropologists and sociologists are engaged in the area of visual ethnography. In anthropology, most of the people use the term "ethnographic film" and some use the term "visual ethnography". The basic practices in both are one and the same.

Anthropological Perspective and Ethnographic Films

Anthropological perspective is the limiting as well as encouraging factor of ethnographic films. According to the nature and subject matter of study, the presentations of the films vary. The dynamic perspective enables to have a dynamic ethnographic film and a narrow perspective limits the film to a different style.

Ethnographic films are essentially art films. When we look onto the so-called "commercial film" and "art film", the connotations of "art film" may be different from the denotations of art film. But, all films are art whether it is commercial film, or art film in contradiction to the various established genres.

Realistic films and unrealistic films can be the two broad divisions to be considered as a set of criteria for the classification. Whether it is realistic or not, the filmmaking is an art hence all films are a kind of art. The so-called commercial films are based on the ingredients put in the film. An "art film" also can be a "commercial film". Therefore, the bifurcation of the commercial film and art film can be based on the realistic or imaginative elements.

The emphasis of ethnographic or anthropological film is based on the scientific knowledge of man and his culture. Of course, man's dreams and fantasies, though it cannot be absolutely understandable by scientific study, are also coming under man's culture, and that itself is art and impetus for art. The depiction of real life, real problems, and the whole reality are the fundamental nature of anthropological films or ethnographic filming whereas the art, artistic imaginations, entertainments, exaggerations of particular events, use of music and songs, etc., are some of the elements in most of our present day commercial films and these films can be generally referred to as an audio-visual presentation of art, literature, and music. Mostly, these films are the product of a linguistic and cultural milieu; nevertheless, there have had some exception for this.

The production of ethnographic or anthropological films is the fast growing areas of interest of visual anthropology. Ethnographic films encompass the scientific research and documentation of culture in visual media. This enables to understand each and every element of the studied and observed elements of culture in such forms and models.

The students or the visual anthropologists study the visual images and the audible aspects and the excellent integration and coordination of these scientifically analysed audio-visual data is the outcome of a study and research, and which can be called as an ethnographic film or anthropological film or visual ethnography.

The production involves the use of the scientific research methods of anthropology and appropriate use of the visual media. The Audio-Visual Anthropologist must have ample knowledge in the use of audio-visual devices (mechanical) and he or she should encode the audio-visual data that will help him to gather the right audio-visual data. Apart from the anthropological scholarship, the visual anthropologist must have the notion of audio-visual communication since the ethnographic filming is a union and montage of anthropological calibre and audio-visual communication.

3

Anthropology and Cinema

The emergence of the discipline of anthropology is based on the urge to understand the existence and development of culture and biology of human societies. Anthropologists, globally, have shown interest in the study of various human societies and their cultures on the one hand and the biological aspects on the other. We, the human beings, are connected to our own surroundings through various ways such as through economic relations, ecological relations, technology, education, kinship, family, marriage, politics, etc. Almost all human endeavours have specific nature or patterns and subject matters. Such specialised areas have been identified by anthropologists and that stipulated in the formation of a number of sub-branches of anthropology and the visual anthropology is only one among them.

The first bifurcation of anthropology has been taken place on the basis of the fundamental aspects of the study, thus anthropology related with man's biology is generally referred to as Physical Anthropology or Biological Anthropology, whereas the other division studies social and cultural aspects of man and that second broad division is called as 'Cultural Anthropology' by the Americans, 'Social Anthropology' by the British, and 'Socio-Cultural Anthropology' by most of the anthropologists throughout the world. Even though, these two broad branches are discarded with its peculiarity in study, there are a number of subdivisions overlaps with the other since man is a socio-cultural and biological species of the animal kingdom.

Physical or Biological Anthropology and Social or Cultural or Socio-Cultural Anthropology are the broader divisions of anthropology. All other branches or specialisations are either belonging to anyone of these two branches or keeping its relation with both the branches.

At present, anthropology is enriched with its various specialisations and methods of study. But it is also realised that a blend of subdivisions are needed in many contexts in order to gather together the knowledge on man. The interrelationships of different subdivisions of anthropology are not accidental, but divided for the convenience and also due to the changes of study in anthropology.

Social and Cultural Anthropology

Social and Cultural Anthropology is considered to be one of the broadest divisions of anthropology and it studies man's cultural and social evolution, development, etc. The study of the origin and development of man through the biological point of view is categorised under physical anthropology, but in contrast social and cultural anthropology exerts its attention in the study of the origin and development of social and cultural aspects of man. The growing necessity of the minute aspects of study of man became a major force in the bifurcation of the discipline and it results in the stipulation of a number of subdivisions for social and cultural anthropology.

Social Anthropology

Social anthropology deals with societies, and social organisation, family, marriage, kinship, economic organisation, political organisation, religion, law, social process, social system, social structure, social change, etc., of primitive as well as modern and contemporary societies.

Some early anthropologists regarded social anthropology as a branch of sociological studies. But, the developments in methodology of social anthropology have uplifted it as an independent discipline. Emile Durkheim's thought had influenced in shaping this discipline. Even so, while discussing on the theoretical developments of social anthropology, Evans-Pritchard, in 1950s, has argued that "Durkheim's importance in the history of the conceptual development of social anthropology in this country [UK] might have been no greater than it has been in America had it not been for the influence of his writings on Prof. A.R. Radcliffe-Brown and the Late Prof. B. Malinowski, the two men who have shaped social anthropology into what it is in England today" (Evans-Pritchard, 1950).

There are many other anthropologists who have contributed to the development of social anthropology and some have attempted to define social anthropology as early as 1870s. The "Founder of Social Anthropology", Sir Edward Burnett Tylor (1871) defined that cultural anthropology is "the study of social behaviour, especially from the point of view of the systematic comparative study of social forms and institutions. The aim of social anthropology has been the application of the inductive method to society. The term was originally applied only to the study of the social organisation of non-literate peoples. Social anthropology has largely been a qualitative discipline."

Evans-Pritchard (1950) says, "social anthropology studies, social behaviour, generally in institutionalised forms, such as the family, kinship systems, political organisation, legal procedures, religious cults, and the like, and the relations between such institutions; and it studies them either in contemporaneous societies or in historical societies for which there is adequate information of the kind to make such studies feasible." In general, social anthropology has some particular views other than cultural anthropology and the debates have narrowed about the concepts and methods of social anthropology.

Cultural Anthropology

The studies on man as a cultural being, his work, behaviour, social patterns, etc., are the main subjects of the cultural anthropologists. "The term culture generally refers to the customary ways of thinking and behaving of a particular population or society. The culture of a social group, therefore, is composed of its language, general knowledge, religious beliefs, food preferences, music, work habits, taboos, and so forth" (Ember & Ember, 1988 : 5). The appellation like 'cultural anthropology', 'social anthropology', 'social and cultural anthropology' are being used alternatively by many anthropologists throughout the world. Cultural anthropology, in the words of Tylor, "is sometimes used almost interchangeably in America for what in England is called social anthropology, reflecting the traditional British interest in social systems and the major interest in culture for American anthropologists." There are some demarcations, however, have been made by the exponents of both social anthropology and cultural anthropology. "Cultural anthropology is the study of the diversity of human ways of life [culture] and the regularities in how culture functions" (Crapo, 2002 : 6).

The emphasis of social anthropology is on "societies" and it is "culture" for cultural anthropologists. The term "culture" was adopted by the nineteenth-century anthropologists. Tylor's (1871 : 1) classical definition of culture views that, "culture or civilisation is that complex whole which includes knowledge, belief, art, morals, law, custom, and any other capabilities and habits acquired by man as a member of society." There are anthropologists like Linton, Kroeber, Beals and Hoijer, and others who have also defined the term culture. According to Herskovits (1955), culture is the "man-made part of the environment." In general, cultural anthropology studies the culture of man synchronically and diachronically, and the subject matter of cultural anthropology is as wider as humanity and culture.

Ethnology

Ethnology is also a term coined for cultural anthropology and it is the study of culture of man on a comparative way. According to Evans-Pritchard (1950), "the task of ethnology is to classify people on the basis of their racial and cultural characteristics and then to explain their distribution at the present time, or in past times, by the movement and mixture of peoples and the diffusion of cultures." Ember and Ember (1988 : 8) says "ethnologists seek to understand how and why peoples today and in the recent past differ in their customary ways of thinking and acting. Ethnology, then, is concerned with patterns of thought and behaviour, such as marriage customs, kinship organization, political and economic systems, religion, folk art, and music, and with the ways in which these patterns differ in contemporary societies." A general understanding on social cultural anthropology is essential for the better practice of visual anthropology and audio-visual anthropology. Visual anthropology is inseparably related to social reality.

Virtual and Converged Reality

The discourse on reality is a critical aspect. "Lecan distinguishes three levels within human reality. The first level is nature, and the third is culture. The intermediate level is that in which nature is transformed into culture. This particular level gives its structure to human reality—it is the level of symbolic. The symbolic level, or order, includes both language and other systems which produce signification, but it is fundamentally structured language" [Dayan, (in) Nichols, 1993 : 441].

The present day developments of audio-visual equipments and computers are capable of generating virtual reality, but the visual media and its electronic and mechanical devices are considerably sufficient to encode and decode the visuality of the culture and biology of man, his environment and both the cultural and physical remains of early man. Here, the gadgets for the documentation are one and the same but the only difference could be traced out in the perspective that rule out virtual reality and converged reality.

Virtual reality may be a computer-generated simulation of reality or it may be an artificial manipulation of events, situation, etc., by the help of modern audio-visual gadgets and also by the artistic use of different events, moments, situation, time-space relations, etc. The converged reality is the reverse of virtual reality. The converged reality is not the reality itself, but a model prepared by the real images, which are encoded from a cultural context.

Realistic Films

Anthropological films, ethnographic films, documentary films, etc., come under this category. Commercial films try to catch the attention of a greater number of spectators and it is structured in such a way to satisfy all the fantasies, dreams and unsatisfied problems of the spectators. Apart from this, the commercial film bears a number of ingredients, which belong to the category of the unrealistic or exaggerated extensions of human culture. These unrealistic expressions are mostly the unresolved desires of common man.

Documentary Films

Documentary film is the factual portrayal about the life and culture of societies. "Documentary film is a motion picture that records news events or shows social and cultural conditions. A documentary is borne out of individual creative art." (David Lowe, quoted in Wolverton, 1987 : 17). According to Hayward (2004 : 90), "The first filmmakers to make what were in essence travelogues and called documentaries were the Lumiere brothers in the 1890s. Thirty years later the British filmmaker and critic John Grierson reappropriated the word to apply to Robert Flaherty's *Mona* (1926). Grierson was the founder of the 1930s documentary group in Britain and was one of the theorists influential in determining the nature of documentary. According to Grierson, documentary should be an instrument of information, education and propaganda as well as a creative treatment of reality." "Although the tradition of recording other cultures dates back to the travelogues made by the Lumiere brothers, it is really Robert Flaherty who was the first documentarist in that tradition" (*ibid.*: 91).

On the basis of the subjects and contents, documentaries are classified into different types, such as news documentary, travel documentary, anthropological documentary, sociological documentary, investigative documentary, explanatory and informative documentary, experimental documentary, historical documentary, etc.

New Wave Cinema

New wave film originally referred to a group of individualistic, innovative, and non-traditional French filmmakers, directors and producers in the late 1950s and early 1960s, including Francois Truffaut, Jean-Luc Godard, Claude Chabrol, Eric Rohmer, and Alain Resnais, who began as critics on *Cahiers du*

Cinema and promoted the principles of auteur theory. "The term New wave was originally coined in the late 1950s by Francoise Giround, editor of the then centre-left weekly L'Express, to refer to the new socially active youth class. However, the term very quickly became associated with current trends in cinema" (Hayward, 2004 : 145). The New Wave film style was characterised by a cinema *verite* style with the use of the jump cut, the hand-held camera, non-linear storytelling, and loose, improvised direction; now used to generally refer to any new movement in a national cinema.

Cinema as an Art

Cinema or Film is an art form, which depicts man's culture in different ways as it does in plays, musical-drama, etc. Film has very distinctive qualities to overcome time and space by its mechanical properties. It recorded or records some aspects of society and culture and it is an effective culture construct or an art form. But, at the same time the very medium, film, can be used to document the observable or visible and audible culture of man with the mechanical device of filmmaking. Thus, there are only two categories of filming. First, culture construct or manipulated culture, and second, the real culture.

Siegfried Kracaurer (quoted in Lehman, 1997 : 107) says "when calling cinema an art medium, people usually think of films that resemble the traditional works of art in that they are free creations rather than explorations of nature. These films organize the raw material to which they resort into some self-sufficient composition instead of accepting it as an element in its own right. In other words, their underlying formative impulses are so strong that they defeat the cinematic approach with its concern for camera-reality." "But in defining them [film] as art, it must always be kept in mind that even the most creative filmmaker is much less independent of nature in the raw than the painter or poet, that his creativity manifests itself in letting nature in and penetrating it." (*ibid.*)

The theory of structuralism, for instance, has its roots in social cultural anthropology and linguistics. Claude Levi-Strauss, a French anthropologist and the "father of modern anthropology", is the champion of structural anthropology. Nichols has rightly pointed out that in filmmaking, "the theoretical premises underlying many of these methods do not originate in film study or even in general aesthetics. They often come from philosophy, linguistics, sociology, anthropology, psychology, Marxism, or phenomenology, and their interdisciplinary blending can be a source of great vitality" (Nichols, 1993).

Film or cinema is a product and it is one of the languages through which the world communicates. Cinema reproduces "reality", which may be the original culture or innovations in culture or imaginations of a filmmaker. The degree of these elements may vary in terms of the policy or politics or ideology of various filmmakers. Film or cinema is framing some facts and fantasies of man and his environment through some particular way and its emphasis varies according to the filmmaker who directs the film.

Film is the art and science of composing and framing of the behaviour and facts to the audio-visual medium with some particular emphasis or other, and the emphasis varies according to the categories of films. All films are art films, but they are not the so-called "art films". The techniques of filmmaking based on science but the style of filmmaking is an art, whether it is an "art film", "commercial film", "documentary film" or an "ethnographic film". All these categories of films are having the differences only in the style and emphasis of filming whereas all these categories of films are based on culture and it is a "culture construct" of man.

Film—Structuralism—Semiotics—Anthropology

In filmmaking, structuralism, semiotics and anthropology are closely related. Anthropology studies human behaviour and culture. Various societies possess specific cultural traits and from which it is possible to understand a particular population. Further, within a particular society itself, one could trace variations. Therefore, anthropological methodology provides a way to understand individual and societal behaviour, which is helpful or essential to portray a filmic representation.

Structuralism has become one of the important theoretical approaches in the study of language, culture, and society. In anthropology, structuralism became vogue with the writings of Claude Levi-Strauss since 1960s. Levi-Strauss's thesis was that since all cultures are the products of the human brain there must be, somewhere, beneath the surface, features common to all. This concept became popular during 1960s and film theoreticians find it useful. It also paved the way for a rethinking of film theories through academically recognised disciplines such as structural linguistics and semiotics.

The introduction of structuralism into film theory was perceived as a bold move to de-romanticise the filmmaker by introducing a more scientifically based approach that could objectively uncover the underlying structures of film. But, it ended up in rigid formalism. Formalism, as a literary theory, refers to critical approaches which analyse, interpret, or evaluate the innate features of a text.

In films, the structuralism emphasis on the particular aspect that how films convey meaning through the use of codes and conventions not dissimilar to the way languages are used to construct meaning in communication. In semiotics, a code is a set of conventions currently in use to communicate meaning. It may be spoken language or behaviour or tone or texture of a visual. Dayan (in Nichols, 1993 : 439) says "semiology deals with film in two ways. On the one hand, it studies the level of fiction, that is, the organization of film content. On the other hand, it studies the problem of film language, the level of enunciation". Film language is a usage to express the intelligible or understandable aspect of a film. Film is considered as a language and it is a way of communicating using visual images and sound. The language of film is based on the visuals, its lighting, tones, editing, sound, etc. The usage "language of film" and language used by man are different.

In anthropology, anthropological linguistics is one of the important branches. "Anthropological linguistics are interested in the role of language in human life...anthropological linguistics are chiefly concerned not with language for its own sake, but with the relationships between language and the human condition" (Crapo, 2002 : 9-10). Language is the most important source of human culture and it is inevitable for an audio-visual anthropological production.

4

Photography and Audiography as a Research Tool

The use of pictures, drawings, etc., in ethnographic reports strengthened the credibility of written records considerably. That is, a "word-picture" combination has been considered to be better conveying; and the use of pictures has been widely adopted as a supplementing thing, which provides additional strength to written records. In this regard, Philip K. Bock opined that "if one picture were really worth thousand words, most ethnographic reports could be shortened to perhaps fifteen pages of plates" (Bock, 1969 : 394). Although Bock's statement is a little exaggerated one, it could be possible to avoid some extra explanations if we are able to substitute visuals to words or sounds or *vice versa*.

Visual Examination in Biological or Physical Anthropology

Visual examinations are being extensively used in biological or physical anthropology as well as in medical science. In physical anthropology, the visual examination and reporting of physical traits, that cannot be measured exactly, example, eye colour, skin colour, etc., have been employed to study and classify races and this visual examination is an important aspect of anthropology.

Use of Still Photographs

Many anthropologists and social scientists have emphasised the use of photographs instead of mere description. Young (1966) argues that the "observers [while conducting research in social sciences] see in terms of their own interests, backgrounds and insights into a given situation. Assume for purposes of illustration that a forest ranger, a lumber dealer, a botanist, and an artist walk together through a bit of forest. The word-description accounting of what each of these four men saw in the same forest at the same time, even if they held themselves to the rules of scientific description, would undoubtedly vary so widely that a fifth man reading the separate accounts would not be aware that the same forest is being described. Such selectivity can be supplemented by the use of photographs. Photographs tend to present accurately a mass of detail, which is apt to escape the human reporter. The photographic 'eye' views with authenticity and impartiality. It has no preconceived notions and selective interests."

The anthropologists like Gregory Bateson and Margaret Mead (1942) have used photography as a research tool, and they portrayed Balinese character through a photographic analysis.

Photography and Audiography as a Research Tool

The audio-visual media and the devices are usually used for teaching, reporting research, and publicity, rather than as a primary research tool. With the advent of portable movie cameras and video cameras, there are a number of attempts which have been made by some anthropologists and many media persons. From the 1970s, video taping of social interaction has become increasingly common.

Video tape has been used as a research tool by Lyn Miles (1976) to examine the sign-language performances and other behaviours of chimpanzees at the University of Oklahoma Primate Centre. At present, many ethnographers, social scientists, educationists are using videos as a tool for research and studies. The advantage of once recorded video or film can play back several times, and this facilitates a researcher to acquire more precision in his research on the audio-visual expression of man and even non-human primates. Apart from this, the recorded materials themselves pave way for further research. Since, there are more chances to have bias of researchers, the real audio-visual data give space for further research and analysis, and it is an advantage. The new perspective Audio-Visual Anthropology ultimately will change the anthropological studies as well as the culture of man.

Although, the documentation and study of audible and visible aspects of man's communication is significant, the good mechanical devices for these are more expensive. The study and recording of audio-visual data may be unaffordable for individual anthropologists, but Universities and other research institutions can provide enough funds for this purpose. Apart from these aspects, the audio-visual anthropologists should have ample knowledge in the use of cameras and sound recorders whereas the policy of audio-visual media is the subject matter of anthropology itself. Despite there may have differences in opinions and perspectives as it had happened when the anthropologists tried to define the term 'culture'. This discussion itself may consider as a piecemeal treatment, nevertheless, this integrated view will make some repercussions in the contemporary studies of anthropology. In this juncture, it is fruitful to listen to the words of Sahay (1993), the author of 'Visual Anthropology in India and its Developments', "the departments of anthropology in various universities should introduce visual anthropology as a part of their curriculum." But, apart from this, I would like to suggest that the anthropology departments should update the anthropological studies by understanding the wider application of audio-visual anthropology.

Prior to the beginning of fieldwork, the researcher should accomplish a detailed study and research on the secondary materials about the subject of study and also about the tools and its peculiarities that is necessary to encode audio-visual data from the field of study.

Audio-Visual Tools

A general idea about the audio-visual tools and their operations are essential for fieldwork and production of anthropological or ethnographic video films in audio-visual anthropology. All these tools are quite expensive hence the fieldwork with these tools is an "expensive fieldwork". The quality of the instruments, however, is based on the price of equipments and low quality equipments are available for low price.

Today, the most popular portable audio recording device is digital voice recorder. It has gained utmost importance in recording conversations, speech, songs, narrations, etc. Researchers, journalists, and others are using extensively this popular audio recording gadget.

Digital voice recorders are quite popular and familiar for many people. Even then, a considerable number of people do not give proper attention to the recording procedures. The apt and careful use of digital voice recorders will help us to enhance and support our knowledge hence the use of digital voice recorders attained extreme relevance in anthropological research, media studies, etc.

By using compact voice recorders, we can record many sounds, such as interviews, narrations, songs, etc. Most of these can record with the built-in microphone. But the built-in microphones are, usually, omni-directional type so that in some situations it may cover unwanted sounds and noise. That is why, in particular contexts we have to attach additional microphones to these recorders, if it provides an external microphone plug-in socket, for capturing better audio.

At present, various types of mikes are available to facilitate recording in different situations. The capabilities of your voice recorder will have to be tested previously before going to the field. The quality of recording is relied on the quality of your equipment as well as the correct placement of microphone towards the source of sound.

Voice operated recording system is designed to start and pause recording automatically to the sound. Interviews can be recorded by a 'voice operated recording' system, but we should not use such system to record songs and the very aspects required to be recorded with its realistic pause, tempo, rhythm, etc.

Still Camera

Photography is used as an effective tool in anthropology and still-photographs are an apt visual substitute to written records. Thus camera and photography became a significant tool of the fieldworker in anthropology. There are various types of cameras available today.

Today, digital cameras have replaced the film based cameras. The digital cameras are easy to use and image corrections and editing are easy with software and computers. The basics of camera operation and the knowledge of picture composition, angles, levels, tone, etc., are essential to make use of photography more effectively in anthropological studies.

Basic Controls and Functions of Video Camera

This part is provided for the beginners as well as those who are not accustomed to the use of video cameras. Video camera is extremely helpful for every behavioural science because video camera is a convenient tool to record audio-visual data of man and his culture. It is interesting that once Jean Rouch, an eminent ethnographic filmmaker opined that "video cameras are toys and an ethnographic filmmaker should use film cameras." But today, the technology has advanced a lot and high resolution video cameras of various brands are available; and the possibilities of the use of video camera have been exploited by many anthropologists, sociologists, psychologists, and others presently. The subjects like visual anthropology, visual sociology, etc., were developed along with the developments of photography, cinematography, and videography.

Today, anthropologists are extensively using photographic techniques to study human groups and their socio-cultural peculiarities. To use a video camera, the following basic controls and functions of a video camera have to be understood as a prerequisite before using it in the fieldwork. 'Operating Manuals' of video cameras provide detailed features of each camera. The maximum knowledge of camera control helps one to use a camera very creatively.

Power Supply

Most of the video cameras can be connected to AC mains by using an AC Adapter and also can run by the specified battery pack.

Operation Switch

Operation Switch is also known as Camera Power Switch. The function of this switch is for turning the Movie Camera On and Off.

Memory Card Slot/Cassette Compartment

The specified type of video cassette has to be loaded into the

Cassette Compartment. In the new generation cameras, instead of cassette, Memory Cards, Hard Disks and Solid State Memory are being used extensively. Memory Cards and Cassettes can be replaced, but the Hard Disks and Solid State Memory are internal and user cannot change them.

Camera/Playback Selector

Camera can be put into Playback mode by this selector switch. In the camera mode, shooting can be done, and in the Playback mode the recorded images can be played back in the viewfinder or on LCD or on to a connected television.

Recording Trigger and Pause Button

In the camera mode, the pause button function as a stop/start trigger and which permits start and stop in shooting a scene. In the Playback mode, the pause button functions as a usual pause button of a Playback.

White Balance Adjuster

According to the nature of light sources, the colour of the objects change, but these changes are not affecting to human eyes considerably because our eyes are adjusting to any situation unlike in camera. Man can see white subjects as white in different lighting conditions up to some extent. But video camera can produce this colour variation in different lighting situation. Therefore, the White Balance of the camera has to be adjusted when before starting any recording. Different lighting conditions like Blue sky, Cloudy sky, Sunlight, Sun rise, Halogen light, etc., are making different colour tones, so that White Balance should be done on every situation. The colour temperature of the light source is measured in Kelvin (K). If the light is more bluish, the

Kelvin value is higher, e.g. Blue sky, Cloudy sky, Sunlight, TV Screen, White fluorescent light, etc., and if the light is more reddish, the Kelvin value is lower. Halogen lamp, sunrise, sun set, candle light, etc., have only lower Kelvin value. The Kelvin value is not directly related to the brightness. In essence, to get recordings with natural colours, it is unavoidable to adjust the sensor of the camera to the existing colour of the light. This is called White Balance adjustment. In several cameras, presets of White Balance are available with an Automatic White Balance option.

Black Balance

Black Balance is available in professional cameras and it is like white balance. White Balance sets the camera reference to true white and the Black balance sets the camera to true black. A poor Black Balance makes unnatural colours in the dark areas of the visual. By adjusting the Black Balance, we can have better pictures.

Iris

The iris of the camera can be adjusted for brighten up the subject when shooting a backlit scene, etc. Iris can open and close. While opening the iris, the brightness of the picture would increase, whereas in closing the iris the brightness of the scene would decrease. In many video cameras Auto Iris is also available.

Electronic Viewfinder

The subject in front of the camera can be viewed through the electronic viewfinder of video camera. An eyepiece corrector is also attached to the viewfinder, and it can be adjusted to the eyesight of the camera operator to have a sharp monitoring while photographing. Apart from Viewfinder, video cameras with LCD screens are available for easy use.

Manual Focus Ring

Manual focus ring permits high precision in focusing to the desired object or subject. Manual focusing is also used for special effects like dissolving the focused image to a blur image by adjusting the focusing ring, and *vice versa.*

Auto Focus

Automatic focus is an advantage of modern cameras. But in certain cameras, the auto focus function is not suitable while recording fast moving subjects because it may create a blur effect.

Manual Zoom-Wide Lever

Manual zoom-wide lever can be used to have quick or very slow zoom or wide functions. In the field situation, usually power is a problem. But manual zoom is optical zoom, which is devoid of power consumption.

Power Zoom Button

Power zoom button makes it possible a gradual and smooth zoom-in and zoom-out function. The speed of this function, however, is usually a fixed one. Whereas manual zoom lever allows us to operate according to our requirements.

In the zoom-in function, the subject appears closer and in the zoom-out function the subject appears as distant. Zoom-in function allows us to record close ups and zoom-out gives wide shot. Zoom-out to zoom-in gives the experience of a wide scene to close up.

External Microphone Socket

In many situations, the use of built-in microphone is helpful to record the synchronized sound with the visuals. High noise is one of the drawbacks of the built-in microphones of most of the cameras. In order to rectify this problem, we can connect various types of external microphones and this can be connected to the external microphone socket. While connecting an external microphone, the built-in microphone will be deactivated.

Headphone Socket

An earphone or a headphone can be connected to this socket for monitoring the recording audio.

Tripod Receptacle

Camera can be mounted on a tripod and the screw of tripod is attached to the tripod receptacle of the camera.

Shooting Pictures with a Video Camera

At first, the power of the camera will have to switch on. Put the camera into recording mode. Then adjust the light setting (White Balance) of the camera, focus the lens, and adjust the zoom also to the desired image of the object. The built-in microphone records the audio, and additional microphones can also be used to obtain desired results. The record-pause trigger/ button permits record and pause functions.

There are a number of different types of video cameras available but the basic features are one and the same. Even though, one should thoroughly understand the operations of the camera, which s/he is taking to the field. Therefore, one has to study carefully the operating manual of the instrument.

Further, this is only a mechanical device and the audio-visual encoding is essentially based on the capabilities of the fieldworker. The shot size, movement of camera, movement inside the frame, consistency, camera level, camera movements, camera angles, etc., are also capable of exerting special meanings to special situations. Finally, photography is based on light and shade, proper lighting or use of natural light is an important thing throughout the visual encoding. Due to the interchangeable emphasis of audio and visual aspects "filmmaking is essentially an art."

If you are not intended to telecast the documented materials, it could be possible to do with minimum expenditure and one can use any handycam.

It should also have to be mentioned that the videos, photographs, songs collected and combined with academic interest may not entertain layman as they have a view of entertainment.

The post-production of a video programme requires a video mixer or a computer with video editing software, audio mixer or audio recording and editing software, audio recorders, monitor TVs, and computers for various graphical presentations.

5

Introduction to Audio-Visual Anthropology

Audio-visual anthropology is a new or an upgraded version of visual anthropology. The history of the development of anthropological studies is also the history of visual anthropology and audio-visual anthropology, which varies from its subjects to the methods. The general tendency of anthropologists are nicely pointed out by Roger M. Keesing (1985 : 1) as "the journey to remote and exotic peoples and places, and back to the present, is the route anthropologists themselves have taken."

Anthropological studies, in the earlier phases, were basically descriptive in nature. Later on, the analytical and interpretative phases followed. In the earliest phase, a number of ethnographic studies came out and ethnography was considered as the base of most of the anthropological studies. According to Bock (1979 : 295) "ethnography is the description of the structure and organisation of single societies" and for Hobel (1972) it is "the foundation of cultural anthropology."

Descriptive anthropological presentation is not devoid of the limitations to include every anthropological notion. This was realised by a number of scholars, for example, Margaret Mead (1936), John Collier (1967), and others. For Chakraborty (1989 : 284) "the details of rituals performed during other ceremonies like first rice eating ceremony, post-funeral function, etc., can be depicted well through photographs of these events stage by stage and then subsequently the ethnographic description may follow... The life and culture of a people can be displayed through photographic album like a silent film with a short annotated description, which may be more impressive and authentic than a simple description of the facts." This shows the transformation of the concept from descriptive anthropology to visual anthropology. A silent film with a short annotated description may be impressive and authentic than a simple description of facts. But, if we are able to provide the original synchronous oral expressions and/ or audio to the visuals, then it will be more understandable than by the former style.

In the 1950s, Herskovits has rightly pointed out the significance of photography and motion picture while discussing written and unwritten tales. Herskovits says that, "one distinction between the stylistic conventions of the written and the unwritten tales must be drawn. The fact that the folk tale is received gives it certain features of the written story can never achieve—just as certain values that the written story are necessarily absent in the tale. These nuances can only be recorded by a phonograph—pauses in speech, interjections, intonation, stress, or by the motion picture—gesture, facial expression and the like" (Herskovits, 1955 : 276).

According to Robinson (1995 : 214), "we live in an age of image based communication, epitomised by cinema ... but we tend to forget how important words are to movies." Robinson further pointed out "there is a parallel between the development of cinema and of writing systems. In order to tell a story, most silent movies were periodically compelled to insert caption cards, printed or hand-written; the images alone could not cope. And of course once 'talkies' were introduced, the silent cinema quickly perished" (*ibid.*). The above statements convey the gradual transformation of descriptive accounts to visual-descriptive and visual accounts. That is, it shows a shift of emphasis from 'language' to 'language and picture'.

Transformations in Anthropological Studies

The earliest attempts were descriptive and it can be referred to as "Text Only Anthropology". Later, anthropologists started to include graphical presentations along with the descriptive accounts. The technological developments helped to provide photographs along with the descriptions and graphs. Further, the use of moving visuals started. Finally, in the present day, it has become a reality to present the audio-visual behaviour of man through anthropological perspective. At present, descriptions or text can be included in audio-visual presentations as oral and/or visuals. That is only why the audio-visual presentations became more powerful than any other means of communication particularly pertains to human interaction. The transformations of anthropological studies can be summarised as follows:

1. Text only anthropology
2. Graphical presentations along with the descriptive accounts
3. Photographs along with the descriptions and graphs
4. Use of moving visuals
5. Use of sounds along with the moving visuals.

Visual Anthropology Vs. Audio-Visual Anthropology

Although, the audio and the visual elements are being explored in anthropological studies, some anthropologists used to put their emphasis merely on visual aspects, which is, at present, referred to as 'visual anthropology'. Makhan Jha (1994 : 157) explains "due to development in science and technology, different types of audio and video cassettes are applied to record folk songs, dances and other details of folklore and lifestyles of the people under study. The scientific development has given rise to this method, which is now known as visual anthropology."

According to Sahay (1993 : 3), "visual anthropology is inextricably connected with photography, whether it be still photographs or films, on the life and culture of various people that are used for teaching, research, feedback, or other applied purposes." Roy and Jhala have tried to provide a definition for visual anthropology in their article, 'An examination of the need and potential for visual anthropology in the Indian social context'. In the words of Roy and Jhala (1992 : 16), "visual anthropology is the study of mankind, employing the camera as one of its main tools. It creates visual text-films and video tapes that celebrate the aesthetics of dance, theatre, music and other arts, it comments on social institutions such as law, marriage, ritual and war, and it occasionally plays the role of an advocate for social change."

The above descriptions and definitions make it obvious that the emphasis on visual anthropology is on visual aspects. The conceptual framework of visual anthropology is not comprehensive due to the fact that the audible element is as significant as the visual element. In many circumstances, to a greater extent, the audible element is inevitable for the understanding of the visual aspects. This is the context onto which I am forwarding this preliminary conceptualisation of a "new version", 'Audio-Visual Anthropology'.

Audio-Visual Anthropology is the study of the audio-visual behaviour of man, and the use of audio-visual equipments to document society and culture is an important aspect of audio-visual anthropology. Video camera, film camera, sound recorders are the equipments and a training in them is also required an anthropologist to become an Audio-Visual Anthropologist.

Communication and Audio-Visual Anthropology

The nature and elements of man's communication is as complex as man is. The non-verbal elements and verbal elements of culture and communication together constitute man's survival in the world. The non-verbal elements and verbal elements of culture can be broadly classified into audio and visual categories of culture. The study of man through this new perspective 'audio-cum-visual' is more important. The blend of audio-visual communication and anthropology is an encouraging perspective and with which it could be possible to make extensive and detailed studies on socio-cultural and biological aspects of man.

The word communication is derived from the Latin word 'Communis' meaning to share, impart, transmit, pass along, make common, or to make known ideas, skills, information or knowledge and so on. Communication is a process in which some information stimulates the perceiver and this process may be active or passive. When man communicates, he shares his own knowledge, attitudes, and skills with others in the form of gestures, spoken, or written messages. "Communication is vital and fundamental to all human survival and is the perception of commonly understood symbolic stimuli of a language or gestures, the verbal and non-verbal stimuli" (Mann, 1980). "Human communication is a process by which we express meaning simultaneously with signs and with symbols. Signs are events such as tears, smiles, clenched fists, or agitated gestures that are spontaneous expressions of our feelings, needs, or concepts requesting little conscious efforts or learning to master" (Crapo, 2002 : 160).

The five elements of the communicative process included in Laswell's model (quoted in Galina 1980 : 88) are as follows:

Act of Communication

1. Who	Communicator
2. Says what	Content
3. In which channel	Media
4. To Whom	Audience
5. With what effect	Effect

Galina (1980) has rightly pointed out that in the communicative process, the transfer of any information is only possible through the use of a system of signs. But the system of signs can be verbal or non-verbal, and accordingly the process of communication can be divided roughly into verbal communication and non-verbal communication.

Verbal Communication

Verbal communication is the communication which pertains to words and its systematic arrangements rather than things, gestures, pictures, etc. Unlike non-verbal communication, verbal communication provides much more precision in conveying the meaning. But, it does not mean that verbal communication is capable of communicating everything since the effectiveness of many non-verbal codes and communication is inconceivable for verbal communication. Therefore, verbal and non-verbal communication imparts a total meaning and both tend to be substituting each other in many junctures in the communicative process. In verbal communication, the transfer of information takes place easily when it is compared with non-verbal communication.

Human speech or verbal communication comprises a system of phonetic signs, which include two principles, viz., lexical (words) and syntactical (the way words are arranged to form phrases and sentences). For Jakobson (1978 : 3), a word, like any verbal sign, is a unity of two components. The sign has two sides: the sound, or the material side on the one hand, and meaning, or the intelligible side on the other. Every word, and more generally every verbal sign is a combination of sound and meaning, or to put it another way, a combination of signifier and signified, a combination which has been represented diagrammatically as follows:

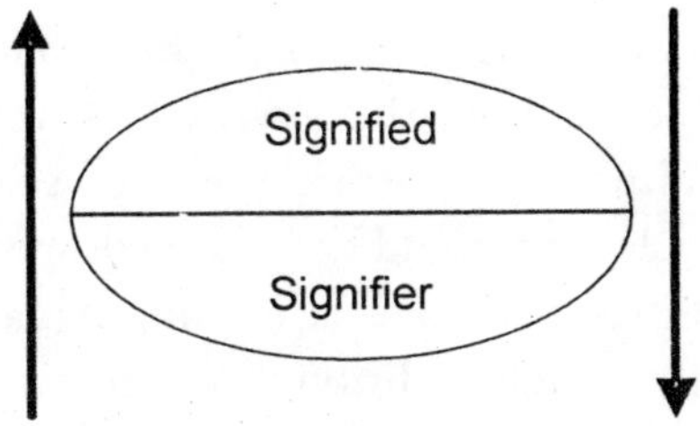

A sequence of sounds can function as the vehicle for the meaning (Jakobson, 1978 : 3). Language is as old as human society and it is a system of arbitrary vocal symbols, used to express communicable thoughts and feelings, and enabling the members of a social group or "speech community" to interact and cooperate. "Language is a part of culture and is socially transmitted. It is basic for culture, as social cooperation without language is difficult" (Tylor, 1871). According to Sturtevant (1947 : 2), "a language is a system of arbitrary vocal symbols by which members of a social group cooperate and interact."

"Language is a media for communicating information by the use of signs, gestures, words, or meaningful vocal sounds. To learn a language, an individual must learn to associate a picture, sound, or symbol with a particular meaning" (Ahuja and Chhabra, 1989 : 15). Herskovits (1955 : 301) has pointed out that, language offers rich resources for his investigations because "the symbolic values of language lead to a comprehension of the latest tangible elements in any body of custom—the values, the goals, the ideals that direct conduct and order convention—while at the same time they reveal some of the deepest roots of culture itself. In truth, symbolisms of this order justify us in regarding language as 'an index to culture', as it has been called; in thinking of it, in the widest sense, as the vehicle of custom."

Paralinguistic and Extralinguistic Signs

Paralinguistic and extralinguistic systems of signs also

supplement verbal communication. "The paralinguistic system is a system of vocalization, the quality of voice, its range and tone. The extralinguistic system includes pauses in speech, coughing, crying, laughter and the tempo of speech itself. All of these supplements increase the semantically significant information not through additional speech information but by 'near-speech' methods" (Galina, 1980 : 90). The study of extralinguistic features of speech, voice tone, pacing, and so forth has become a part of the traditional work of non-verbal research.

Non-verbal Communication (Body Language)

Non-verbal communication is also known as body language. Non-verbal communication plays a greater role in the communicative process and it is a supplement to verbal communication. Every non-verbal system of sign aid in revealing in full the semantic aspect of information is referred to as non-verbal communication. According to Galina (*ibid.*), "the system of non-verbal communication involves its own system of signs, which can be considered as a definite code." For Mann (1987), "non-verbal communication is a sort of communication in which presentation codes are used and the communication is carried out through body language." During interpersonal communication and group and societal communication we receive a stream of non-verbal information. "Affiliation, sexual attraction, rejection, aggression, dominance, submission, appeasement, fear, grief, and joy are known to be expressed extensively through non-verbal communication" (Mann, 1980 : 13).

The codes of non-verbal communication consists bodily contact, proximity, orientation or angular position, appearance, head nodes, facial expression, gestures or kinetics, posture, eye movement or eye contact. Apart from the codes (system of signs) to convey messages, non-verbal signs exhibit some meaningful expressions. It is also providing additional quality or support to the verbal communication. Dress, gait, touch, skin colour, body figure, eye colour, lips, eyebrows, hair style, closed fist, arrival time, fingers, blushing, perfume, facial features, tone and pitch of voice, etc., are some of the non-verbal stimulators.

All human expressions other than verbal communication are referred to as non-verbal communication. Verbal and non-verbal aspects have quite a significant role in conveying messages in different or the same social situation. Pike (1993 : 33) has provided an example according to which intentions or wishes can be made explicit in a sentence like *I wish you would close the door.* Or, they can be made explicit in a statement like *The door is open and I am shivering,* where the hearer knows (by deduction or experience) that the speaker wants him to close the door. In the case of non-verbal expression, the above actor could pretend to shiver strongly and then gesture towards the door. Thus the hearer can understand the intention of the actor.

Morton Wiener (1972) have pointed out that the accurate interpretation of gestures is very difficult because "similar movements may serve different functions and different movements may serve similar functions." Some communication theorists opined that the system of signs or codes are supplementing to verbal communication only when the participants understand completely the signs and codes used in the communicative process. In general, in verbal communication, the system of signs using speech and in non-verbal communication the system exhibited through unspoken signs.

In essence, in verbal communication the system of signs uses speech and in non-verbal communication the system exhibits through unspoken signs. Therefore, verbal and non-verbal elements of culture of man can be broadly classified into audio and visual categories of human interaction between man and man and also between man and the environment. The audio channel of the encoding equipment records every possible audible element of human communication whereas the visual channel of the encoding equipment encodes every visually observable aspect of man. The following chart is an example for some of the probable correlations of audio and visual data.

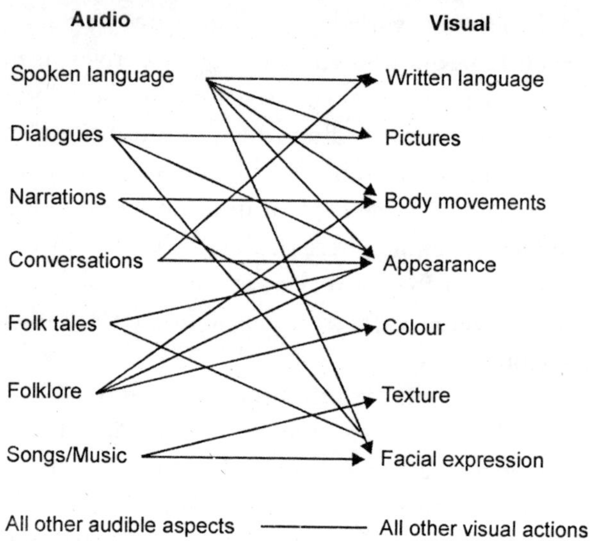

Ethnographic filming is the audio-visualisation of the languages and cultures, whereas ethnographic films are the audio-visual records, which can be used for the purpose of research, study and analysis.

Similar to visual anthropology, ethnographic filming is also an important area of audio-visual anthropology. In ethnographic filming too, there are only two means to include every cultural and linguistic domain. In ethnographic filming, the visuality, kinesics, proxemics, a number of non-verbal aspects, etc., can be recorded through its visual domain. John Collier, the author of 'Visual Anthropology: Photography as a Research Method' (1967), has rightly mentioned that "only the moving picture film can record the realism of time and motion, or the psychological reality of varieties of interpersonal relations (quoted in Pelto & Pelto, 1978). Facial expression, body gesture, body movement, position, mutual body orientation of the speakers, etc., communicate some culture-specific meanings and these proxemic, kinesic and non-verbal elements can be recorded in film or videos. On the audio channel, every paralinguistic aspect can be recorded along with speech. This dual capacity may provide valuable information whenever we analyse the ethnographic films of the vanishing and/or vanished cultures and languages. In general, ethnographic films encode the "actual behaviour" in either case of language and culture. It is not intended to encode the things in its abstract level.

Some have differentiated language and speech; for instance, in the words of Bock (1979 : 53), "speech is the actual behaviour, whereas language is the set of rules (categories and plans), which explain the regularities observed in speech. Each person who learns a language ... must infer the rules of language from the sample of actual speech." If this is an acceptable fact, the audible element of an ethnographic film may also be suitable for the recording and preservation of changing and/or vanishing languages. The visual part of the film, on the other hand, can provide the style and context of the act. The audio-visual coverage of ethnographic filming is uniting the social context of speech through some visuals and its influence upon speech. Besides this, ethnographic films can provide primary data more faithfully than any other means or method. Due to these peculiarities ethnographic films are invaluable for anthropological studies. The effective combination of audio and visual provides a new conceptual framework and because of the shift of emphasis of the perspective, it should be perceived as 'Audio-Visual Anthropology', a new version of 'Visual Anthropology'.

The Blend of Audio and Visuals

Empirically, the equivalent for the audio and visual perceptions is the information expressed through eye and ear. "The eye gives information about shape, colour, surface qualities, and motion of objects in three-dimensional space by registering the reactions of these objects to light. The ear reveals little about the objects as such; it only reports on some of their activities, which happen to produce sound waves" (Arnheim, 1958 : 156). But in many instances, visuals are incapable of providing the as such meaning and it is unlike verbal responses, so that the blend of the qualities of eye (visuals) and ear (audio) has become indispensable to understand every complexity of man.

The visuals and the representations of visuals are essentially like that of a cultural system of symbols. In the words of Schneider (1968), "a cultural system is a system of symbols. A symbol ... defines as something which stands for something else, or something else, where there is no necessary relationship between the symbol and that which it symbolizes." According to Mann (1987), "some have even considered language as the most important of system of symbols. However, they do include painting, music, literature, arts, drama, etc., as other parts of such a system." Language, however, has been stressed more for the reason that human beings represent symbol-making and symbol-using species, and it is among them that symbolic communication exists, and hence the existence of culture.

Arnheim (1958 : 180) has rightly pointed out the distinction between visuals and words. "There is a recognizable difference between the literary description of visual action and attempts to describe in words something to be produced visually. In the latter case, as we know from the technique of the film scriptwriter, words are used as a mere expedient. When a poet describes a painting, the result is not a painting, and it is not intended to be one. On the other hand, an attempt to fixate with words a piece of visual action, simply because no other means of recording is available, will easily turn out to be absurd literarily and to make excessive demands on the visual imagination of the reader, even though the description may come from a gifted writer."

From all these instances the distinction of audio or audible elements of man's communication and non-audible aspects, that is visual elements of understanding, have been expressed their effectiveness in man's cultural interactions. These elements dominate all other elements in several instances. The significance of audio and visual need not be exaggerated because in understanding every human expressions like conversations, story telling, songs, narrations, folk tales, folklore as well as in participant and non-participant observations; and in all behavioural studies, it has already been recognized the relevance of audio (audio recording) and visuals (recording the visual images) for the studies and analyses.

From the 1950s itself some anthropologists like Herskovits pointed out the necessity of audio-visual recording methods in anthropological studies. Herskovits (1955 : 276) says that, "one distinction between the stylistic conventions of the written and the unwritten tale must be drawn. The fact that the folk tale is recited gives it certain values that the written story is necessarily absent in the tale. These nuances can only be recorded by a phonograph—pauses in speech, interjections, intonation, stress, or by the motion picture—gesture, facial expression and the like. Oral literature, that is, as the instrument of the able teller of tales, is dramatic in form."

Besides the plans and proposals regarding the use of audiography and photography by a few anthropologists, some have paved the way for practical experimentations and the efforts of Flaherty, Margaret Mead and Gregory Batson are monumental, and it is considered as the earlier efforts in which the potentialities of audio-visual tools and its methods employed.

In general, the verbal and non-verbal aspects are categorised into the audio and visual information, and this perspective is the fundamental nature in communicating a greater part of anthropology, hence Audio-Visual Anthropology underscores its relevance today.

All visuals are behaviours or symbols and they possess obvious and definite meanings as well as every sound (audio) create some definite messages. That is the visuals and audio are providing significant elements in any behavioural study. It can be asserted that no behavioural scientist can study anything without the help of audio and visual expressions. Man visualised his ideas through sculptures, pictures, drawings, writings, etc., other than oral disclosures. For instance, when we look on to the sculptures, pictures, or drawings we would find that it is the absolute product of the understanding of man's visual perception on some thing else. Man sees something and perceives something where there is a process taking place in between man and the object of perception, which is visual communication. In this visual communication, the whole universe is an object of perception. Every visual stimulates and creates some modifications in man's knowledge. When we confine our objectives to visual behaviour or element, and sounds of men, we are underscoring the significance of Audio-Visual Anthropology.

Earlier some anthropologists like Gregory Bateson and Margaret Mead, and others realised the relevance of photographic techniques in anthropological studies. Apart from this, some anthropologists attempted to document man's culture in audio-visual media. The ethnographic filmmaking, documentary making, research filming, etc., are also made with the reliance of audio-visual media. In all these instances, the excellent fusion and integration of anthropological calibre and audio-visual media were taking place. Thus anthropology has got one more diversification and that discipline is presently known as 'Visual Anthropology'.

Although the audio and visual elements are being used in anthropological studies, most of the anthropologists were emphasizing merely on visual aspects. Jha (1994 : 157) explains that, "due to development in science and technology, different types of audio and video cassettes are applied to record the folk songs, dances and other details of folklore and lifestyles of the people under study. The scientific development has given rise to this method, which is now known as visual anthropology."

According to the 'Journal of Visual Anthropology', publishing since 1978, "Visual Anthropology promotes ethnographic filming, the use of media in cultural feedback, and the development of Third World ethnographic media productions." The journal also provides space for discussions of the study, use, and production of anthropological and ethnographic films, videos, and still photographs for research and teaching. Further, its interests are in the analysis of visual symbolic forms from a cultural historical framework; the analysis of the structuring of reality as evidenced by visual productions and artefacts; and the cross-cultural study of art and artefacts from socio-cultural, historical and aesthetic points of view.

Some anthropologists have had realised the relevance of visuals and audio in anthropological studies and filmmaking. Even though most of them are using the capabilities of the audio and visuals, it seems to have given more emphasis on visuals.

Photographs or Visuals

It is a widely accepted fact that photographs cannot lie, as we get a more realistic idea of the world around us from pictures than from words. But a photograph or visual, in some instances, may not be completely intelligible, and this deficiency emphasise on the need of illustration. Certainly, "a picture is worth a thousand words." A picture leaps into the mind and feeling more quickly and directly than words. They are the culture itself, instead of the abstraction of culture that words represent. Although some pictures are worth a thousand words, there are some words too that are worth a thousand pictures. Some say that, a picture is worth a thousand words only when some words accompany it. As a consensus to this argument Louis Alexander (1987) says that, "there are many things pictures can do that words cannot. But there are also some things that words can do, that pictures cannot. The best possible situation is a combination of pictures and words—a word-picture partnership." Printed words being visual representations of spoken words, and the sense of hearing is basically related to the act of reading. According to Wilson Hicks, "man, in understanding what happens around him, depends primarily on his sight, secondarily on his hearing" (quoted in Ahuja, 1992 : 330).

Although visual anthropology is relatively a new branch of cultural anthropology, since long before anthropologists used to reconstruct the replicas of art forms, material culture and even the anthropomorphic forms by drawing, or making the models or replicas by the use of some moulding materials. In this regard, the interest of anthropologists in visual aspect of man and his culture could be traced back to the onset of the discipline anthropology itself.

Visual sense attained and entailed some significance in our life. Earlier, man used to make pebble tools and in the first stage he was bothered only in making sharp cutting edge on the tools, later on he began to make some aesthetic additions on the tools. Engravings on the walls of his rock shelters or on the walls of caves may be his first artistic works. According to many archaeological-anthropological reports, there are many drawings, carvings, engravings, rock paintings, etc., excavated throughout world. From these excavated materials, the physical anthropologists have told that man's stereoscopic vision is also an important factor in making those art forms and the very thumb of man itself pave way for the present man-machine relationship and the study of man-machine relationship is called as ergonomics.

Observation limits the understandings to overt levels of analysis. A photograph for instance, in which a man is sitting near a table and there is a pen, a writing pad, and a book near to him on the table, but his eyes are closed. Now, what could be perceived from such a scene? This photograph is providing some possibilities of understandings and some may perceive it as the man is thinking while reading, whereas some others may say that the man started sleeping after reading some time. In both of these possibilities we get entirely different meanings. That is, the same visual segment creates different meanings in different individuals.

One possibility can be the continuation of some other possibilities. We are all observing overt behaviours and most of the observations of anthropologists involve common sense categories of actions at the most overt and explicit levels of analysis and the units of analysis are relatively broad, whereas some anthropologists have focused on the less conscious and overt expressive bodily behaviours and on symbolic use of spatial relationships. The focus on details of bodily movement is often referred to as Kinesics. In the words of Sharma and Bhatia (1989), kinesics refers to the study of bodily language or communications by gestures and bodily positions and movement. The study of social symbolic uses of spaces was labelled as proxemics by Edward T. Hall. Proxemics and Kinesics involve such fineness of observational detail that special training is required in the terminology and notational system by which gestures, postures, touches, and other bodily motions can be recorded.

The behaviour or visual of the man from the above said instance could be learned empirically through the visual medium. The methods of observation also come under the arenas of interests of audio-visual anthropology and visual anthropology. In fact, all visual aspects come under the area of interest of every anthropologist.

In order to understand the necessary aspects of the minimum definable element of culture, it is necessarily to have an in-depth study of the visuality of objects, images, behaviours, etc., and it is a must to comprehend and elucidate culture.

All objects, images and behaviours possess some meanings and this act as signifier and signified, and at the same time the visual of these aspects entail some particular visual extensions and it is nothing but the elements which are interconnected in some way or some other way. The position of the element in the nexus of culture is unique and particular, and the study and the explanation of these observable or visible aspects have been equally interesting for visual anthropologists and cultural anthropologists.

Visual anthropology is referred to as the cultural study of visual images and which comprising the artistic drawing of early man to the culture of contemporary man too. The historic materials and the artefacts are providing only the visual elements and it can be perceived visually, whereas the present ethnographic films are providing a mass data of the audio-visual elements of culture and the visual anthropologists are also analysing the audio-visual data but their major concern is visual data. In this situation, I would like to put forward a strong emphasis on the new perspective to understand the audio-visual expressions of culture and communication with the hope that with which it could be possible to study culture as a whole. The emphasis has been shifted from visual to audio-visual and this is the base of audio-visual anthropology, a novel branch of holistic anthropology. Audio-visual anthropology studies audio-visual behaviour of man and advanced audio-visual equipments are inevitable to pursue this sub-discipline.

There is one another question also to be answered. Is it possible to communicate completely the culture of man through the audio-visual elements? The first-hand answer is "no", because man has particular and distinctive sensory channels through which he understands about his environment. Vision (visuals), hearing (sound/audio), touch, taste, smell, etc., are man's sensory channels among these we anthropologists generally make use of the possibilities of two perspectives and by which it could be possible to study the after effects or motivations of their sensory channels too.

As far as a visual is concerned, it is an element, which is perceived by man's communication channels like vision, hearing, touch, taste, and smell. Every human communication is facilitating through these five faculties. Of course, we all know that vision, hearing, taste, smell, and touch are our five senses; but it is also said that in addition to touch, the skin contains separate warmth, cold, and pain senses (Morgan, 1956). Kinesthesis (muscles tensions) and the vestibular sense are other senses and in total the number of human senses is nearly ten than five. Certain tissues of human body, where transduction take place and these are all man's senses. In order to understand about the world around us, the process of converting physical energy into nervous-system activity, that is transduction, is an essential process to be taken into consideration. So, it is indispensable to know the significance of our sensory channels and the sensory process in relation with human behaviour and experiences. It is through our vision (visual) and sounds (audio), we anthropologists perceive a major amount of information about man's culture. However, hearing probably second only to vision as channel through which we can learn about and appreciate our world. Through hearing, we can understand speech and we receive a great many signals and cues. Therefore, the understanding of our sensory channels and the elements, and the theories of man's communication are important and relevant for those who are interested in the Audio-Visual Anthropology, which is firmly adhered to various theories and methods of anthropology.

Although the eyes and vision are not an indispensable factor of human communication, the power of the sensory channel—vision bears the foremost position in man's interactions with the world around him.

Smell, for instance, is another sensory process through which we experience the proximity of odorous substances. Smell has a significant role in controlling man's behaviour and up to some extent smell can resume the memories of past experiences. A pleasant smell and a bad smell create different experiences and accordingly some difference in behaviour and it can be perceived the visuality of behaviour exerted by the sensory process smell. In this way, generally, we can perceive and study the culture of man through the audio-visual elements, because it can include the other cultural behaviour or expressions which come out as an effect from the causes like touch, taste and smell; and these behaviours can be recorded into the audio-visual media. Accordingly audio-visual anthropology could cover man's culture comprehensively and truthfully. By this novel version, 'Audio-Visual Anthropology', we can accomplish the study of culture, visual images and more comprehensively it studies the visual and audible aspects of culture and culture construct.

All kinds of communication, viz., visual, audio, touch, smell, and taste reveal the fact that communication is always the realisation of definite relations or associations or exchanges of the above five elements. Through these sensory perception or sensual communication, man communicates to the other man whether he is a layman or a social researcher. The levels of communication, however, may be different namely, inter-personal, intra-personal, group level and mass level. The communicating elements like visuals, audio, smell, taste, and touch have inseparable nexus in human communication and through the audio-visual anthropological view, we could study and analyse every audio-visual element of man's socio-cultural interactions.

During communication or man's interaction, people exchange various proposals, ideas, interests, moods, emotions, etc. All of these can be considered as information, allowing the process of communication to be understood as a process of the exchange of information. In the five sensory faculties of man, the audio and visual faculties have more prominence in group level and mass level communication and also in anthropological and sociological researches. The visual faculty, for instance, is the basis of the methods of observation. Whether it is participant observation or not, there the anthropologists observe and scrutinize the behavioural culture and its symbols by using the researcher's own visual faculty and he can make use of a mechanical device to observe and record the necessary moments or sequences of that particular culture. The still photography enables the researcher to capture important moments, whereas a movie camera or video camera enables him to encode some relevant moments and its sequences of a culture in the audio-visual media.

In essence, this example reveals the significance of the audio and visual sensory skills of man. The other sensory faculties like touch, taste, and smell have greater significance in inter and intra personal levels of communications, however, as such it cannot be taken into consideration while discussing about audio-visual anthropology. But it could be possible to translate the audio-visual behaviour of touch, taste, etc., by depicting its corresponding cultural behaviours. In other words, as far as Audio-Visual Anthropology is concerned, the expressions or behaviour originated by the sensory process can be studied with its audio-visual behaviour. In this regard audio-visual anthropology covers a greater level of understanding than visual anthropology. Audio-visual anthropology put forward a new methodology of perceiving all audible and visible elements of man for encoding and decoding culture with its realistic ambiences and models. Apart from this, the precisely encoded audio-visual materials provide ample scope for further research and analysis.

Definition for Audio-Visual Anthropology

"Audio-visual anthropology can be defined as the study of audio-visual behaviour of man and the use of audio-visual media to document man's culture is an inextricable aspect of audio-visual anthropology" (Mahendrakumar, 1997 : 49 and 2007 : 55). Here, in this definition, the phrase "the study of audio-visual behaviour of man is the pivotal aspect of the new version, audio-visual anthropology.

Major Areas of Interest of Audio-Visual Anthropology

Audio-visual anthropology and the nexus of its ideas are mostly derived from social and cultural anthropology. However, audio-visual anthropology, in turn is capable of contributing its methods to socio-cultural anthropology and to physical anthropology. Some major areas of interest of audio-visual anthropology are as follows:

1. The cultural study of visual images and man's behaviour.
2. Study and analysis of audible aspects of culture.
3. Ethnographic or anthropological films.
4. Use of audio-visual anthropological methods in media analysis.
5. Use of audio-visual anthropological methods in anthropological studies.

Cultural Study of Visual Images and Man's Behaviour

The cultural study of visual images covers a wider perspective and some of the instances are namely, the study of historical materials, museum specimens, archaeological finds, artefacts, agrofacts, art, craft, sculpture, drawing, carvings, paintings, cultural symbols, technological profiles, and all other observable aspects or visible culture or overt behaviours or visual images of man's culture comes under this category. In general, the very research and analysis are also based on the theories and scientific research methods of anthropology. The synchronic and diachronic analysis also required and the archaeological anthropological notions, art, aesthetics, historical knowledge, etc., are valuable for the cultural study of visual images.

The minimum definable element of culture is called "culture trait" (Kroeber) but the study of a culture trait should be done from its real context and the separation of any trait from its real environment make the study meaningless, but how can we study and elucidate this since we know that the signifier and signified are different like something which stands for something else, where there is no relationship between the object and its explanation. In order to reduce and rectify this discreteness of signifier and signified, the reliance and inclusion of audio-visual factors in anthropological studies are inevitable. And the research and analysis of the audio, visual and audio-visual media are anew with its exceptional capabilities from the last half of the 20th century.

Scientific Study and Analysis of Audible Aspects of Man's Culture

Scientific study and analysis of audible aspects of culture is an important perspective in audio-visual anthropology. So far audible aspects of man did not gain a momentum in anthropological studies, despite some scholars have studied the folk songs, folk tales, narrations, etc. The cultural study of audible aspects of audio-visual anthropology extends its scientific analysis on a number of things and some of them are listed hereunder.

Folklore, folk tale, narrations, oral history, dialogues, conversations, music and songs, sounds and ambience, speech, etc., of culture and cultural milieus.

Herskovits has rightly pointed out that "the word 'folklore' was first employed in a letter signed by Ambrose Merton, published in The Athenaeum of London, August 22, 1846. "Its writer, who used this pseudonym for his real name, William J. Thomas, urged that accounts of "the manners, customs, observances, superstitions, ballads, proverbs, &c. [etc.] of the olden time" be recorded so that later students could turn for information to these dying remnants of the unrecorded past that were termed "Popular Antiquities, or Popular Literature" (Herskovits, 1955 : 272).

At present, the study of folklore, folk songs, folk tales, narrations, etc., are considered to be the areas of interest of folklorists and historians, however, earlier, some anthropologists have made extensive efforts in this field and many folklorists are using anthropological methods and theoretical basis in the study and analysis of folklore.

Anthropologists and folklorists have made some comments on the pitch of music and of folk songs, while discussing about the different aspects of 'Ethnomusicology' in a National Workshop on Ethnomusicology held at the Department of Anthropology, Calicut University Centre (now the Department is a part of the Kannur University), and this workshop was sponsored by the Central Institute of Indian Languages, Mysore, Karnataka. High pitch and fast rhythm of music shows the intensity of emotional state than low pitch and slow rhythm.

In general, there are some scattered and segmented ideas developed among some scholars, but it is not yet emerged as an integrated one, and the very integration and study of man's cultural expression could be made possible under audio-visual anthropology. The scientific study and analysis of audible aspects of man's culture is to emphasise the audio element of our culture and this is an indispensable subject of audio-visual anthropology. This will strengthen the new division of anthropology by illustrating the visuals with the as such audible elements of man and his environment. Audio is effective in strengthening and substantiating any visual. That is, the reliance on covert or overt behaviour is incomplete whereas the behaviour or visual substantiated with audio is more understandable. In short, the decoding process of the encoded behaviour synchronised with audio become easier other than mere visuals and *vice versa*.

It is also observed that many anthropologists and folklorists have made a lot of descriptive study about folk songs, folk music, etc. Although there are excellent methods to depict the audible aspects like the use of music manuscript, use of audio tapes or discs, etc., most of the attempts are confined to mere verbal writing. This has to be changed and the audio-visual anthropologists must find ways to record them in the audio-visual media. In the print media, we can make use of music manuscript to depict the songs in the as such rhythm and scale and the printed materials can be stored for centuries unlike the digital media. The audio-visual anthropologists, for example, could record some classical songs, folk songs, tribal songs, etc., on the digital voice recorders. Then, one can do the following things:

1. Type down the lyrics of songs;
2. In the next step, the music manuscript of each lines of songs can be provided;
3. And in the last phase one can describe all the meanings, relevance, history, peculiarities and the research findings could be made under the head 'the scientific study of audible aspects of man's culture'.

The visualisation and the above said aspects are integrated in the major areas of audio-visual anthropology, that is, in the ethnographic films or anthropological films. This necessitates an excellent blend of audio and visual aspects of man's communication, and it is an expression of his learned culture that provides the real moods, emotions, temperament or the psychology of man and the descriptions and interpretations are mere 'signifiers'. As Malinowski said, the study of culture trait unless it is in the real context will be meaningless. Similarly, more abstract representations about a socio-cultural milieu will restrict the observer of a culture from its empirical arena. Hence, the selection and elimination of print format or visual format or audio-visual format is as important as the anthropological research.

Interviews and verbal responses are audible elements of man's culture. Through an interview, one gets only verbal responses, and the discrepancy between verbal responses and actual behaviour is well recognised in social research. If we want to understand behaviour we need to observe the unit of study of a given situation. What we can get through verbal responses is attitudes and values or the likely behaviour and the perceptions of behaviour.

The audio element is inevitable and inseparable from audio-visual anthropology since it can provide a substantial level of information like narrations, dialogues, and its various moods. The use of music and songs in films, dramas, etc., provide moods. Say for instance, if you are watching a film or a drama, you could see some visuals and could hear the audio, that is, music and/or dialogue that give some particular meaning, hence the right audio provides more meaning to a visual. But, the misuse of audio can reduce the mood of a visual. Quite often we are experiencing artistic or strategic use of audio in most of our cinemas.

Some voices or sounds or music are capable of making a nice experience to the audience. Although there are some technical problems in recording original audio from the field situation, it is better to use the maximum possible, original and contextual audio in anthropological films.

Music is an extension of man's artistic talent and up to some extent it makes some particular emotional setting, however, the use of alien music in films make the whole film an effectively manipulated artistic work, not a realistic profile of culture. Of course, literature, art, music, etc., are having its own separate areas and much more research and activities are taking place everyday, despite some anthropologists have had touched these subject matters in connection with anthropological studies.

Audio-visual anthropology is firmly attached to anthropology and audio-visual elements of culture and society. We cannot separate anyone of these elements from the framework of audio-visual anthropology. This firm and inextricable or fused characteristics of this scientific sub-discipline is rather anew by its distinctive qualities and methodology under the holistic anthropology.

Significance of Visuals and Audio in Understanding Culture and Society

In the words of Pelto and Pelto (1970), in the social sciences, most primary data come from three sources: (1) directly observing human behaviour, (2) listening to and noting the contents of human speech, and (3) examining the products of human behaviour particularly those products found in archives, museums, records and libraries. Here, the "human behaviour" and "products of human behaviour" primarily come under the visual categories and speech pertaining to the audible element. The study and/or encoding of these audio and visual categories of man are the mainstays of audio-visual anthropology.

Empirically, the equivalent of the audio and the visual perceptions is the information experienced through the eye and the ear. "The eye gives information about shape, colour, surface qualities [texture], and motion of objects in three-dimensional space by registering the reactions of these objects to light. The ear reveals little about the objects as such; it only reports on some of their activities, which happen to produce sound waves" (Arnheim, 1953 : 156). In many instances, visuals are incapable of providing the exact meaning and are unlike verbal responses so that the combination of the qualities of eye (visuals) and ear (audio) become indispensable to understand every complexity of man. Thus, all behaviours of man can be categorised into two major divisions such as audio and visual. In every mode of human interaction, namely interpersonal or group level or mass level, man bears the position of an observer and/or receiver and/or sender of information. These characteristics are undoubtedly common to all and all these modes of communication take place mostly through the audible and visual categories.

Asen Balikci (1992 : 176) has rightly pointed out the relevance of audio-visual media. Balikci says "Visual anthropologists assume that audio-visual forms of expression and communication play an important ideological role in society and that they can be appropriately used for purposes of cross-cultural understanding in a world divided by xenophobic feelings." All these instances points out to the significance of audio and visual in the understanding of society and culture.

6

Fieldwork in Audio-Visual Anthropology

Fieldwork is the mainstays of anthropological research. Fieldwork and empirical analysis are inevitable and the collection of primary data is possible only through fieldwork. The fieldwork in audio-visual anthropology is mostly based on the audio and visual data, thus the tools to collect this data are also important besides various anthropological research methods. Hence, the students or disciples of audio-visual anthropology must have ample knowledge in the use of audio-visual equipments.

As far as the cultural anthropologists are concerned, it requires a minimum technological possession with him to launch his research and studies. The cultural or social anthropologists can gather ample data from the field without much technological reliance. It requires some scribbling pads, paper, pen, audio recorders, etc., to record necessary field data like conversations, oral history, narrations, songs, tales, etc., and apart from this the use of a still camera provides him/her to capture required visuals from the field of research, whereas the fieldwork in audio-visual anthropology has some distinctiveness than the conventional anthropological style of research.

It requires some additional prerequisites in Audio-Visual Anthropology than the usual style of data collection because the data collection in Audio-Visual Anthropology is mostly with the audio-visual systems, and the fieldworker must have ample knowledge in the use of the equipments, but at the same time he should avoid distorting the objects of study. In order to gather as much data as the researcher required can be encoded by the well-known and simple strategy—"going native", but with an audio-visual tool.

In Audio-Visual Anthropology, one has to be equipped with good gadgets to collect cultural behaviours, besides detailed observation methods. Moreover, the researcher must also have some basic notions in operating the audio-visual equipments. Some of them are described hereunder.

Pen and Pad

Written language can record descriptions of people, places, and things. It can record speeches and it can explain who, what, why, where, when and how. The only material needed is a pen and writing pad. The 'pen and pad' note taking is difficult in many situations and this could be ruled out by the use of modern gadgets like voice recorders, cameras, video cameras, etc.

Digital Audio Recorders

The use of conventional Tape recorders have almost stopped and today Digital Audio Recorders are popular, with which one can record the exact words of speech, interviews, songs, folk tales, and other sounds in good quality.

Anthropologists began to use tape recorders during fieldwork from the end of the 19th century. After the IInd World War the magnetic tape recorders came into existence and it helped to record more or less a large amount of conversation from the field.

Cameras

With the help of a good camera, we can record the visual images of people, events, actions, and things. That is, in essence the use of camera helps to encode or preserve the behavioural culture on some formats. For example, photographs are visual records to show how people, places, actions, or things looked at the time of recording.

When a combination of writing, tape recording, and camera is used, total information can be gathered. Today, the video cameras are a convenient tool for audio-visual anthropologists. We can record enough visuals with its real ambience and sound from the context and milieu of culture where we conduct fieldwork. To make it possible, we have to have necessary gadgets wherever we go or to whom we observe, since the depiction of such behaviour is impossible through the medium of written language.

High Definition Film Style Digital Camera

Of course, it is quite encouraging for the anthropologist to use video cameras for the research. Thanks to inventors of low light sensitive digital video cameras. Today, medium sized and portable cameras are available, which can be easily taken to the field. Some of the video cameras are very user friendly in comparison with Cine Cameras and sound recorder, because these are not so cumbersome. Apart from this, the low light sensitive cameras give better results even from the indoors or low light situations. This enables the researcher to avoid the use of extra light and if it is necessary, one can use the minimum lights to boost up the brightness of the scene. But we should remember that the use of lights would definitely distort the psychology of the ordinary people or tribes, at least for a while, for they are not experienced actors or actresses. This distortion may make some obstacles in the data collection.

As far as an audio-visual anthropologist is concerned, the video camera is a convenient tool, and with which one can record enough visuals with its real ambience and sound from his field, even if there are some technical limitations. In this juncture, I would like to suggest that an audio-visual anthropologist must have the audio-visual gadgets along with him throughout his fieldwork. The audio-visual raw data gives an empirical experience, nevertheless, the data analysis, the explanations and interpretations of research findings also should be provided to illustrate the visual images and also to organise the audio-visual anthropological research report and/or the ethnographic film.

Apart from the Digital Still Camera, Digital Voice Recorders, and SD (Standard Definition) video cameras, the anthropologist can make use of the HD (High Definition) or AVCHD (Advanced Video Coding High Definition) cameras too and these formats provide extremely good visuals. It is important that the students or exponents of Audio-Visual Anthropology must get some training; only then one could use these instruments properly. Certainly, it is a widely accepted fact that "most anthropologists are not experts to operate the audio-visual equipments, whereas the filmmakers are either uninterested or not known about anthropology is a dilemma" (Sahay, 1993). But the effective attempts will definitely enable one to be an expert in both these aspects and becomes an asset to the discipline of Audio-Visual Anthropology.

Even though Audio-Visual Anthropology is considered to be a novel version of Visual Anthropology, its interests are as broad as anthropology and the very audio-visual media and the tools are the backbone of this novel branch. Further, this inextricability and peculiarity cannot be compartmentalised since its scope and subject matter is as holistic as anthropology.

In ethnographic film, we should provide necessary narrations apart from the depiction of primary audio-visual data. But, in certain cases it should be possible to avoid narrations of anthropologist's or interpretations to a greater extent for the primary data may itself exhibit the meaning. In the descriptive ethnographic account of observable culture or visual images, it should provide with enough visualisations or pictures or photographs along with the descriptive account.

The Audio-Visual Anthropology performs the cultural study of visual images, where the audio may be silent. But, while making ethnographic film, one should observe and study the realistic aspects as scientifically as possible and should depict such behaviours with such ambience and audio.

The description of an ethnographer may not be enough to understand the as such picture, whereas the audio-visual materials will provide as such forms or cultural behaviours and this would enable everybody to understand the realistic things. Repeated analyses of audio and visual images are possible with the audio-visual equipments and this enriches the Audio-Visual Anthropology and it is an advantage of this new sub-division of anthropology.

Limitations in Anthropological Filmmaking

Anthropological filmmaking has some limitations. Although anthropological films must be the scientific study and documentation of culture in audio-visual media, at all time the audio-visual anthropologists may not be able to record the real life situations in the very moment when it occurs, because all cultural behaviours are random expressions and not a continuous activity just like our random memory and diverse behaviour patterns. Sometimes, we have to request the people to repeat the very cultural expression once again for filming, and special care should be taken when we persuade people to repeat a cultural expression.

In documentaries and docu-features, the filmmaker is filming the exact situation and expressions, which deserves more audio-visual anthropological significance, whereas the manipulated story, visuals, actors, scenes, culture cannot be considered for the analysis of ethnographic film analysis; but it can be taken for the study of man's creativity or art and thus it is related with anthropology and audio-visual anthropology. Obviously, the present day films/movies are based on man's culture but a combination of effectively manipulated human expressions and they are the creations of man. Audio-visual anthropology, however, studies art and culture and particularly the audio-visual element of man's cultural expression, in this way films such as "commercial films" and "art films" are also having some significance.

The film industry, at all time, similar to many institutions and industries have become a culture area where diverse combinations of cultures and expressions are occurring. By keeping in mind the theoretical model building of Claude Levi-Strauss, films can be considered as a model constructed from the elements of some raw data of diverse cultures. However, some films are accepting the real cultural traits of a cross-section of people or some real life traits. The visuals and the audio of films are quite relevant for the research and analysis in Audio-Visual Anthropology.

The history of filmmaking, its trends, developments, impact of film on society, the relations of technology—culture—cinema, etc., are some of the topics for in-depth study. The anthropologists should come forward to undertake the task of producing audio-visual anthropological films, videos, still stories, slides, drawings, audios, and the collection and preservation of museum specimens apart from written documents, descriptions, records, etc., to enhance the scientific study of man. Anthropologists, folklorists, and many others are studying folk tales, folklores, narrations, conversations, songs, etc., and they try to reconstruct the past events and culture.

The story telling behaviour is quite human, so we cannot criticise the imaginations and stories of a filmmaker because he uses his own style of expression through some stories or fictions, it may or may not be true, but it may be based on his understanding about the world, people and its total ambience. When we analyse the "commercial films", we come to know that the cultural traits are one and the same, but normally we are searching for the scientific study of culture, in that way the commercial or fiction films provide some elements of culture as well as creativity. That creativity part, of course, is coming under the discussion of art, literature and anthropology.

In anthropological studies, many eminent anthropologists have lived in the midst of particular cultural milieus and provided a bulk of ethnographic and ethnologic materials. The pioneers were attempting to depict the culture and behaviour of some people and their culture. At the same time, there are many stories, fictions, novels, poems and in general a number of literary works which have been published throughout the world. Obviously, the characters in these literary works were men and women, but do we consider it as anthropological works or can we come up with a scientific explanation based on the analysis and study of these works. Since these works are related with man's culture, it could be possible to get a vague or partial profile of the real life, and it cannot be taken for a perfect understanding of culture. In literature and art there are many schools of thought like romanticism, expressionism, impressionism, naturalism, etc. Say for instance, the exponents of naturalistic tradition were depicting the pictures of all subjects in its real colour, style, texture, etc., whereas the ethnographic studies provide a realistic and descriptive study of culture of man.

Of course, there are limitations for words. Arnheim opines that, "there is a recognizable difference between the literary description of visual action and attempts to describe in words something to be produced visually. In the later case, as we know from the technique of the film scriptwriter, words are used as a mere expedient. When a poet describes a painting, the result is not a painting, and is not intended to be one. On the other hand, an attempt to fixate with words a piece of visual action, simply because no other means of recording is available, will easily turn out to be absurd literarily and to make excessive demands on the visual imagination of the reader, even though the description may come from a gifted writer" (Arnheim 1958 : 180).

Audio-visual anthropology stresses its emphasis on empirical knowledge on the audio and visual behaviours of man. It is an expression of man by which man communicates each other. The data collection or encoding of the audio-visual data should be done most carefully without destroying the real behaviour of man and his culture.

Compared to many other disciplines, methods of observation in anthropological work require a very little measuring and observing instrument. In anthropology, the main instrument of observation is the fieldworker himself. All other mechanical instruments are the supplementing devices, which help the fieldworker to sharpen his perception; and the mechanical devices store data in its recordings.

7

Audio-Visual Anthropology and Development Studies

Audio-visual anthropology can be used extensively in Development studies. For instance, Sathya Mohan P.V., an Indian Visual Anthropologist, has made a few visual anthropological films, and his 15 minutes film entitled 'Tribal Displacement' points out that the construction of the Polavaram Dam Project on the river Godavari in Andhra Pradesh will devastate the tribal habitats and about two lakhs tribal people will be displaced under the Dam Project. The project is estimated to submerge for hundred villages and four thousand hectares of forest in Dandakaranya. We must also consider various developmental activities of our government, which are intended to enhance the quality of life of the people of India. This film portrays the problems of an important development project of India. Of course, audio-visual anthropological approach is capable of imparting a lot of positive things with its applications.

Applications of Audio-Visual Anthropology

At present, there are three major areas of application of Audio-Visual Anthropology. They are: (1) Research and Study, (2) Reports and (3) Awareness Programmes. These three areas can further be divided into the following categories:

1. Research and Study

1.1 Documentation has the first priority
1.2 Study of Vanishing Cultures and Languages
1.3 Synchronic Studies
1.4 Diachronic Studies
1.5 Comparative Studies

2. Reports

2.1 Making Audio-visual reports based on Research Projects on Development Issues. (Much liberal approach has to be made in order to gather sufficient audio-visual data. The limitation of this method is that it will be time and money consuming.)

3. Awareness Programmes or Educating People

3.1 After conducting need-based studies or for introducing a new programme for the development. (Caution: appropriate audio-visual anthropological presentations have to be made use of in order to educate people.)

Limitations and Advantages of Audio-Visual Anthropology

It is an accepted fact that cultures and languages are changing gradually or abruptly according to the pace of socio-cultural change, and this has attracted many anthropologists and linguists. In every life-situation each culture trait is correlated with a particular word, a phrase or a sentence. Each society has a set of customs and practices comprising the culture complex, which is associated with certain pattern of usage in particular languages. Also, it is obvious that the prevalence of language is firmly connected with the prevalence of culture, and change of culture makes some effect on language and *vice versa*. Therefore, the documentation of vanishing cultures and languages is an inevitable area of study.

Although, audio-visual encoding or ethnographic filming is a tedious and expensive programme, the appropriate use of this method would give us a lot of audio-visual data by which the researchers can examine the material and it can be used for making films. It is also an advantage that the audio-visual recordings or records provide permanent data and opportunity for cultural and linguistic analysis. Moreover, the films/videos may be better kept in the audio-visual repertories of anthropological research centres.

Despite film and video are the essential formats to record the audio-visual behaviour, the DVD and Blue Ray Disc are good means to preserve the documented aspects for a long time.

The digitization of these audio-visual data would help the anthropologists to make extensive studies in the coming decades. According to Joel Birnbaum, chief scientist at Hewlett Packard (quoted in Tapscott, 1995 : 96, 97), "digitization means that all information, including audio and video content, can be used in any order and can be rearranged at will. Digital content can also be transformed for use in another medium—for example, from text to voice or vice versa." Digitization enables interactivity and it provides for computer-based application too.

Audio-visual anthropology just like Visual anthropology will never become a danger or threat to the traditional people, as it was discussed in the International Seminar on Visual Anthropology organised by Anthropological Survey of India in collaboration with Indian National Trust for Art and Cultural Heritage (INTACH) at Jodhpur, Rajasthan in 1987. One of the recommendations pointed out that, "the dangers of visual anthropology to traditional people fixing them as exotic isolates, perpetuating colonial attitudes." Visual Anthropological or an Audio-Visual Anthropological document is primarily an anthropological work. It is unlike fiction. The year of the production of a film has greater significance too. The synchronic perspective, the diachronic perspective, the emic and etic view of cultures and languages must be considered in analysing an Audio-Visual Anthropological document and/or a Visual Anthropological document.

Therefore, an Audio-Visual Anthropological document will not become a threat to the people. On the contrary, it will assist the government in better understanding the needs of the people whose development it embarks upon. If we are going to make obstacles in the process of the development of the people, it is quite sure that the people will discard the very activities of anthropologists.

As far as the matter of subjectivity and selectivity are concerned, they are one and the same for every anthropological account. Therefore, it will be a futile attempt to find problems in the matter of subjectivity and selectivity either in Visual Anthropology or in Audio-Visual Anthropology.

Finally, we will be able to provide all the truth through the audio and visual aspects of culture. The abstract level information or idea could be provided in audio-visual anthropological presentations by the aid of graphical presentation as well as audio. Thus, with the audio-visual anthropological presentation it will be possible to reduce the limitations of visual anthropology as well as descriptive anthropology.

In conclusion, the verbal and the non-verbal aspects are categorised into the audio and visual data or information. The audio and visual aspects of culture can be documented according to various applications. Audio-visual anthropological perspective can encode the vanishing cultures and languages of man. In an audio-visual anthropological presentation, there is no need of "description—visual—description—visual" types of work as found in an ethnographic report. Audio-Visual Anthropology is also eclectic in nature similar to its maternal discipline.

Thorough technical knowledge as well as ample practical experience is needed to pursue Audio-Visual Anthropology. Moreover, Audio-Visual Anthropology has a unique capacity to linger with its virtual reproductions.

8

Audio-Visual Anthropology and the Problems of Tribes

The study and research of the problems of the tribes have been one of the major areas of interests in anthropology. Till date, there are a number of scholars worldwide who have studied about various aspects of tribal life and culture. Anthropologists, Sociologists, Psychologists, Economists, Historians, Linguists, and others have made extensive studies and still continuing it on the various problems of tribes. As their perspectives and accentuations are diverse, the outcome is also different. Most of these attempts, however, are materialised predominantly by the use of languages, numerals, and some photographs. But, the use of audio-visual anthropological methodology is helpful to delineate and portray the problems of the tribes with perhaps a "realistic" manner and it may be more fervent, which makes the studies maximum intelligible unlike the descriptive ethnographic type of elucidation.

The perspective of Audio-Visual Anthropology and the present-day developments of audio-visual instruments are intertwined. The term "realistic" is a relative term and all it depends on the researcher's special skills in using the audio-visual instruments; and the encoding must be done without artificial acting and stylisation since such artificial behaviour is likely to mask the natural or normal traits of the subject and object.

Tribal communities and their problems are diverse and this chapter, however, highlights some of the problems to provide a general background, which is perhaps supportive to portray the tribal problems through the methods of audio-visual anthropology.

Tribes are living in every country. Their problems vary from habitat to habitat and from country to country. As these people have lived as a marginalised population of the world, they suffer from a number of fundamental problems. The technologically, economically and educationally poor or illiterate people of the world may not be able to compete with the majority of any nation; for the majority used to fix all the points for their own interests, and this may probably stipulated in the neglect of the minority. This division is known differently, such as tribes, aboriginals, backward people, minor ethnic groups, little community, etc. But, Behura (1996 : 1) says, "the word 'tribe' has not been defined anywhere in the Constitution of India. But it states in Article 342 that the Scheduled Tribes are 'tribes or the tribal communities or parts of or groups within tribes or tribal communities', which the President may specify from time to time by public notification. As these communities are presumed to constitute the oldest ethnological segment of the Indian society, the term 'Adivasi' ('Adi' means oldest and 'vasi' means inhabitant) is commonly used to designate them. The International Labour Organisation Convention 107 held at Geneva on 5 June, 1957, classified these people as indigenous."

Indian Tribes

India has the second largest concentrations of tribal population in the world. African continent is in the first position. In India, the tribes constitute a significant percentage of the total population and the problems of these people are one among the problems of India. According to the 1991 Census, the total

Scheduled Tribe population in India is about 6.78 crores which constitutes about 8.08 per cent of the total population of 83.86 crores in the country, excluding the population of the state Jammu and Kashmir where Census could not be operated for the disturbed situation. According to 1991 Census, there are 427 Scheduled Tribe communities in India with a population of 6,77,58,380. According to 2001 Census, there are 461 tribes and the population of them is 8,43,26,240. Of these, 74 tribal groups are categorised as "primitive tribal groups". Das (1996 : 337) says, "the 'primitive' tribes have been identified in Bihar, Orissa, Tamil Nadu, Andaman and Nicobar Islands, Madhya Pradesh, Andhra Pradesh, Gujarat, Maharashtra, West Bengal, Karnataka, Kerala, Rajastan, Tripura and Uttar Pradesh. These 'primitive' tribes are technologically and educationally most backward. They, therefore, deserve more urgent attention."

The tribes in India show a great deal of variation, and they possess some particular customs and practices, besides this they have special languages or dialects. Khubchandani (1992) says that "language of India belong to four different families: Indo-European (Indo-Aryan and Dardic sub-families) 74 per cent to the country's total population; Dravidian 24 per cent; Austric 1.2 per cent. The entire population speaking Austric languages is classified as tribe. Tribal languages in other families account for: Tibeto-Burman about 80 per cent, Dravidian nearly 3 per cent and Indo-Aryan little over one per cent."

The tribes are believed to be the earliest settlers in the Indian peninsula and are generally called *Adivasis*, implying original inhabitants (Mahanti, 1994 : 11). In the words of Bhowmick, "tribal communities...called aboriginals or autochthones they are a very backward section of the Indian society, and the earliest types of civilisations are attributed to their ancestors. But due to various historical processes of stress and strains over centuries, and to advent and invasion of various more powerful ethnic groups from outside, they had to retreat for safety and shelter into the inhospitable hilly and forest regions of our country to eke out their existence somehow. In course of time, they developed a spirit of isolation and consequently narrow worldview leading to strong in-group feeling" (Bhowmick, 1980 : 60).

A number of scholars pointed out that these indigenous people have developed successful practices of resource management and land use patterns, such as hunting, gathering, fishing, shifting cultivation, terrace cultivation, nomadic pastoralism, herding, etc. It is also pointed out that some tribal groups possess extensive knowledge of herbal medicine, soils, plants, animal and climate. But, most of the tribes knew little about the world outside or what was or is happening there.

After Independence, the Central and State Governments have attempted to develop a system of education including primary, secondary and higher education throughout the country. Education of the tribes has exerted a tremendous influence and the very education and political awareness are giving them a sense of identity with their fellow countrymen. Some anthropologists have explored the problems of education in the tribal areas.

The problems of educational development in tribal areas are complex and they vary from one region to another. The common problems include economic backwardness, poor attendance and ineffective performance of teachers, inadequate educational incentives, lack of encouragement, isolation, a uniform system of medium of instruction, lack of infrastructure facilities and financial constraints. The economic backwardness is closely interrelated with their education. The Scheduled Tribes children substantially contribute to their family income through assisting their parents in the various economic activities like looking after the livestock, house, children, and grown up children and the agricultural activities. This phenomenon is common in all tribal areas where the tribal economy forms basically a subsistence mode. In such circumstances, the children are bound to discourage the educational facilities provided by different agencies, which leads to high drop-outs at all stages, absenteeism, stagnation and wastage of school education (Venkadesan, 1996 : 28).

An average tribe today is despondent, many of them on the verge of becoming split personalities not knowing where to belong. His abandoned existence and lost heritage compels him to seek ethnic resurrection... He is becoming more vocal about his ethnic identities and is gradually expressing a desire to retain his regional and territorial boundaries (Mehta, 1996 : 64). Moreover, denial of independent social status for the tribes has created some repercussions.

Some have rightly underscored on this issue of the social status and the socio-cultural factors of the tribal problems. Mahanti (1994) says, "the Scheduled Tribes are distinct ethnic groups without any stigma of untouchability or hierarchical inferiority. Some Indian writers, however, have presented a very distorted account of their social status. They have not only denied an independent social status to the tribes but have described them as 'Backward Hindus'. This amounts to assimilation of tribes into dominant Hindu society. Such approach will lead to extinction of tribal culture, religious beliefs, traditions and lifestyle and would obliterate all distinctions between castes and tribes. The tribes are very much agitated over such approach. They are fully aware of the plight of the untouchables even though untouchability has been abolished and would not like to become one of them." Moreover, in many instances the "Tribes" do not receive even a mere consideration of a "contemporary man". The vested interests of the "mainstream" are still persisting through the use of the words like "primitive", "aboriginal", "savage" or "backward", etc., to refer to the educationally, economically developing "contemporary man".

Consensus and arguments are still continuing in many aspects appertains to the problems of tribes. Since Indian Independence, the government have been trying to improve the tribal condition, but they still continue to be most "backward". This is a question that needs careful consideration—how can we bring these people into the mainstream of life? At the same time, some ethnologists feel that their (tribes) integration with the rest of the community will result in the loss of their identity. According to them, the tribes should be allowed to come out a separate life and encourage them to follow their traditional ways and culture.

It is obvious that the tribes are at various levels of social, cultural and economic development. In India, the tribal areas are generally situated in inaccessible areas and sparse population, livelihood based on non-wood forest produce, etc., are characteristic of the tribal areas. The problems arising out of these circumstances are multi-fold. Mann (1980) has highlighted some problems of Indian tribes as follows:

1. Some problems are basically inherent in the life of the tribes who have been conditioned, to a great extent, to face them. Eco-systems of varied forms regulate their way of life and the associated problems thereof.
2. Certain customs and traditions in tribal culture have, directly or indirectly, contributed a great deal to the creation and continuity of some problems.
3. Illiteracy and ignorance of the tribal people have been taken advantage of for exploitation and other ends of similar nature.
4. Many problems arose under the situation of culture contact, specially with caste Hindus and others who got settled, at various stages, in the tribal areas.
5. Unsystematic approach of administrative and other officials, in many cases and specially in the past, has caused hardship in certain areas of tribal life.

All interactions and developmental programmes create some functional displacement among every population and a transient disturbance on the existing system may occur or in some instances it acts as an indispensable consequence. But in many societies or communities, these shifts are creating some sort of cultural shock and it emerges out as different problems. In certain cases, some general developmental programmes make adverse effects among tribal as well as non-tribal people. According to Vyas (1980), displacement of people, due to construction of dams, is a nation-wide problem. Since Indian Independence, a number of dams have been built specially in tribal regions and the rehabilitation became a task of the state. The State Governments realised that payment of compensation did not end the responsibility of the State. The displaced people need to be rehabilitated to lead a new life of economic prosperity. The experience of displacement, caused due to major dams, shows that displaced people were given cash compensation and were left to shift for themselves. There has been no follow-up action on the displaced families. There is growing realisation now, that it is not enough to award compensation, and that the State Governments should assume responsibility for rehabilitation of the displaced people, rendered homeless and landless.

The National Forest Policy as well as Wild Life Protection Act of India and its amendments have curtailed the liberty of the tribes in the use of forest. The forest policy was introduced by the colonial government in 1894, and after Independence the Government of India redefined it in 1952. This has been amended again in 1988. As a result of the new forest policy, the tribes have lost all rights in forest. This has created some fundamental issues as they were absolutely depended on the forest for their whole life. In fact, the economy of the Scheduled Tribes is mainly based on forest and agriculture, and because of the deprivation of tribes from right in forest and the unauthorised alienation of tribal land, the tribal economy is in the crucible today. Mathur (1977 : 93) suggested that special legislation should be enacted to protect the interests of the tribes on land. He further argued that "mere passing of law is not sufficient and loopholes have to be plugged whenever they exist. Otherwise this would enable the unscrupulous exploiters to defeat the purpose of the law."

Exploitation, it is a fact and factor, which could be observed throughout the world, and the general pattern is exploiting the weak. In India, the history of tribal exploitation varies from feudal to the new class. The traders, merchants, money-lenders, etc., have chartered their fetters among the tribes and the ignorance and poverty made them as helpless as possible, this is the covert activity taking place in the exploitation of tribes. The economic exploitation by the money-lenders with their "shady methods of accounting" is a crucial matter that has completely ruined the tribes. These money-lenders succeed in ultimately depriving the tribes of "everything" they have.

The exploitation varies from wealth to lust. The screams of unwedded mothers are reverberating in many tribal areas, but there is not any measure without loophole to stop this "unwanted population multiplication". Some have also reported the exploitation of tribal women. Deogaonkar (1990 : 93) says, "... tribal women who are poor, ignorant and move out of their homes as farm or forest labourers. A tribal woman has a cultural background due to which she mixes freely with the men—particularly before marriage. She is also curious and shows interest in the new things. The relationship between men and women, boys and girls is extremely healthy and free—devoid of all perversities and distortion. Their dress is also peculiar due to tradition. Outsiders who include some officials, roving merchants/traders, truck-drivers, contractors and their labourers brought from outside mis-interpret the women's behaviour and try to make advances. At times the poverty of the women or her curiosity is also exploited for the satisfaction of carnal desires."

In terms of tribal development, the Government have proposed and implemented a number of activities and they are continuing them to uplift the people from the "innumerable" problems. "The welfare programmes undertaken to ameliorate their lot are designed in such a way as to raise their socio-cultural, economic and educational status to level attained by the dominant sections of the population in the State, within a reasonable period" (Mathur, 1977 : 121). But even today, the tribes continue to be most backward in spite of the Government have been trying to improve their condition. Three decades back, while discussing the problems of tribes in the hilly tracts of Gujarat, Lal and Solanki (1976) opined that "it is a common sight in these hilly areas to find families eating edible roots, leaves and fruits and flesh of hunted animals during the lean period of about two to three months. This is a clear indication of the failure to take the benefits of development to these people."

Whether activities of development are taking place, the tribes experience a severe discrimination from many angles of interaction; and a majority of the tribes even started to show some symptoms of psychic stress. The very discrimination persuading them to disappear inside the forest and becoming incapable to come up with the "mainstream". At the same time, in some areas, tribal discontent, agitation, Naxalite formation, etc., are emerging and these are treated as big issues. But, how these issues are coming up—is not a fundamental question for the government for a long. According to Deogaonkar (1990), "in fact, the Naxalite problems should be treated as a by-product of the socio-economic problems of the tribes and not as a purely law and order problem." Besides this, leadership vacuum has also adversely affected tribal development, and vested interests have not allowed tribal leadership to emerge. This factor is one of the important causes of discontentment among the tribes (Mahanti, 1994 : 26).

For the development of the Scheduled Tribes, various planned efforts have been made since Independence. In 1950, the Constitution of India modified and enlarged the scope of such arrangements, considering the tribes specific needs of protection and development. Constitutional safeguards came into force on 26 January, 1950. The Article 46 makes a laudable claim that, "The State shall promote with special care the educational and economic interests of the weaker sections of the people and, in particular, of the Scheduled Castes and all forms of the Scheduled Tribes, and shall protect them from social injustice and all forms of exploitation." The Constitution provides various safeguards in favour of Scheduled Tribes. These may be broadly divided into two parts such as one for the Protection and second for the Development (particularly economic development). Protection of interests of Scheduled Tribes is very essential for their development and the provisions for which are made in the following Articles. Article 15(4), 16(4), 19(5), 23, 29, 46, 164, 330, 332, 334, 335 and 338, 339(1), 371(A), 371(B), 371(C), Fifth Schedule and Sixth Schedule. Provisions relating to development of Scheduled Tribes are contained mainly in Article 275(1) and 339(2).

Today, it seems to be so strange that even after 60 years of Indian Independence, the tribes in comparison with other sections have benefited least. This is fundamentally for the reason that the other sections of the society are highly organised and capable of establishing their voice in front of the rulers. And ultimately their voice is heard and they enjoy benefits. But, the stigma of "aboriginality" and "primitiveness" given to them by "modern society" has already created them as handicapped as possible for not to walk with the "mainstream" or onto "mainstream". In many parts of India, the tribes have long been remained silent in spite of a few have made some agitations and movements.

The application side of the audio-visual anthropology may be helpful to let their voice be heard and which is proposed as one among the tasks of this novel sub-discipline of the holistic science of man.

It is a vital point that the future development of any human group can be planned only after collecting necessary basic information. This viewpoint has been accentuated by many anthropologists, and the consensus about this idea is quite fervent today. Development requires identification of problems and resources, definition of goals and framing strategies for the efficient use or resources to achieve these goals (Pattanayak, 1976 : 245). According to Belshaw (1977) (quoted in Rao, 1988), "development represents an increase in the capabilities of the society to organise for its own objectives and to carry out its programmes more effectively." Rao (1988) says "any plan for development envisages a reorganisation of existing relationships of the members of the particular community for which the development plan is intended for." Any plan of action that is designed to modify the living condition, economy, education, health standards, etc., becomes failure unless it is based on the necessary basic information. It is inextricable that all basic information has to be obtained prior to the planning. Socio-cultural and psychological aspects have to be taken into consideration without any disagreement; this would be definitely helpful to prepare a successful plan of action.

In fact, there is a growing realisation that development process in order to be enduring and of a lasting benefit to people have to be rooted in their cultural traditions. A development model cannot be transplanted in an alien cultural situation. It has to be internalised and woven into the cultural norms and behaviour of the people. To this realisation anthropological studies have contributed most (Kapoor, 1996 : 77). It requires an objective study detailing the population size, literacy level, subsistence pattern, land use pattern, occupational categories, level of dependence on forest resources, type of property holding, traditional political organisation, impact of outside contacts, utilisation of modern communication devices and environmental degradation to have a thorough understanding of the ground situation in each tribal pocket (Sudarsen and Xavier, 1996 : 114-115).

The process of development attempted through the planned change in a society is conceived by anthropologists as a dimension of social or cultural change of the society (Rao. 1988 : 16). One of the preoccupations of anthropologists is to study the social framework of particular society or community as reflected in the beliefs, values and attitudes to access the potentialities for change and anticipate consequences in the process of planned change (*ibid.*). At the same time some (For example, Deogaonkar, *et al.*) say that it is the high time for the Government to create an atmosphere in which the officers working at the grass roots level can freely and candidly give their real impressions, views, suggestions and the policy planners ought to accept their comments or at least not victimise them lest they may again start giving false pictures flattering the Government views and approach.

Anthropologists concern for people and their methodology of field investigation ensure anthropology a place in the social and life science, which is unique. These two aspects of anthropology also ensure that it will remain relevant to public policies and programmes dedicated to people's welfare forever (Kapoor, 1996 : 71). Applied anthropology could find out appropriate remedies whereas Audio-Visual Anthropology could depict all necessary background information, and the amplitude of audio-visual anthropology will become a 'notebook', which carry every information of tribes as well as non-tribes and in general all problems of mankind. Apart from this, Audio-Visual Anthropology can be used as a background for the developing people and society wherein it could be possible to show the problem facing people that how do some other societies overcome their problems, is an advantage of Audio-Visual Anthropology, and it will exert great changes and this new sub-discipline has far reaching prospects.

APPENDIX- I

Visual Anthropology and Audio-Visual Anthropology: A Model Syllabus

Course Objective

The Indian society is changing very fast from its oral tradition and folk art medium to modern society. Similarly, the tribal, rural and urban societies are also under quick changes. The technical advancements of Visual Anthropology and Audio-Visual Anthropology are a boon for the students of anthropology and they should be in a better position in comprehending and projecting anthropological dimensions and dynamics of people of India. The objective of the course is to provide ample training in Audio-Visual Anthropology so that students can acquire a better understanding of society and culture.

Unit 1. Visual anthropology: concepts, scope, uses and problems.

Unit 2. Introduction to Audio-Visual Anthropology.

Unit 3. Ethnography and Ethnographic Films.

Unit 4. History and development of visual anthropology.

Unit 5. Visual anthropology and Cinema: commercial, realistic, new wave cinema, and documentary films. Television and Visual Anthropology.

Unit 6. Audio-Visual Anthropology as a mode to preserve culture and as an input to cultural enrichment.

Unit 7. Audio-Visual Anthropology as an aid to development programmes.

Unit 8. Audio-Visual Anthropological Film review, appreciation and criticism. Film as an art. The film language.

Unit 9. Scope of Audio-Visual Anthropology in India. Its uses, urgent problems and future possibilities. Necessary conditions for filmmaking.

Unit 10. How to produce Audio-Visual Anthropological films and videos.

APPENDIX-II

Branches of Anthropology

This appendix is included for the beginners as well as those enthusiasts who want to study Visual Anthropology and Audio-Visual Anthropology. A general understanding on anthropology is needed for the beginners and enthusiasts to have better works in Audio-Visual Anthropology. Anthropology is the study or science of man and it is a very broad subject. An outline of some specialised topics is included here to have a comprehensive view on anthropology. The word anthropology has originally been derived from two Greek words 'Anthropos' and 'Logos'. Anthropos, meaning man and logos means study or science.

The phrase "study or science of man" gives only a vague outline of anthropology and it is rather a blanket usage, not a clear-cut description despite it seems to be. This problem has been virtually resolved through the rhetoric use of the prefixes like cultural, social, medical, physical, psychological, economic, ecological, etc., along with the root word anthropology. The application of any kind of logic in analysing the meaning of anthropology may be futile than stretching the meaning of various profiles of anthropology today. At this juncture, it would be positive to discuss the various perspectives, which gave shape to the holistic study of man.

Anthropology is the universal science of man. The subject matter of anthropology is as vivid as the man and the universe. Man and his existence and interrelations to other genus and species, and the environment together constituting the subject matter of anthropology. The fission and fusion of areas of interests of the students, scholars, disciples and exponents of anthropology are still continuing. A number of sub-divisions have been emerged while some of them have fused together too. This is the context on to which I am presenting a new version of anthropology, referred to as Audio-Visual Anthropology, to make the knowledge more scientific and realistic.

Till date, many anthropologists have extensively discussed the meaning and areas of interests of anthropology. Nevertheless, before to give an introduction to Audio-Visual Anthropology, a succinct introduction of anthropology will be helpful for the readers to have a comprehensive view of the subject and it will in turn help to understand the new branch Audio-Visual Anthropology.

The first bifurcation of anthropology has taken place on the basis of the fundamental aspects of the study, thus anthropology related with man's biology is generally referred to as Physical Anthropology or Biological Anthropology, whereas the other division studies social and cultural aspects of man. This second broad division is called as Cultural Anthropology by the Americans, Social Anthropology by the British, and Socio-Cultural Anthropology by most of the anthropologists throughout the world. Even though, these two broad branches are discarded with its peculiarity in study, there are a number of sub-divisions overlapping and appertains to each other since man is a socio-cultural and biological species of the animal kingdom.

Anthropology studies man's biological, cultural, social, psychological, economic, political, and historic traits from the prehistoric to the present times of the tribal, rural and urban societies and his sub-human and pre-human origins apart from concerning itself vary vitally about our own lives. That is, in general, the science anthropology covers a wide range of aspects concerning with man and it is generally agreed by every scientist that all men living today belong to a single genus and species,

Homo sapiens, and that all men are derived from a common stock. But, we are all programmed by our own traditions to do something and also not to do something.

Culture is acquired and it is a powerful means for controlling human environments exactly because it is not biologically inherited. For instance, nobody is born able to speak, read, and write any language. Children have to be taught speaking, reading, and writing. From the very example, it is obvious that the essential thing about culture is that it has to be acquired by each individual by learning from others; and it is not transmitted from parents to offspring through the sex cells, as is biological heredity. Further, man alone adapts himself, in a large part, by actively or even deliberately changing the environment, and inventing and creating new environments.

According to Tylor (1871), "Anthropology : The study of man. The word probably originated with Aristotle's description of the man with lofty ideas who is not a gossip or a talker about himself. The word anthropology is first found in English in an anonymous book on human nature, which divides the subject into psychology and anatomy. In the modern sense of the word, it is found in Hundt's *Anthropologeion* (1501), dealing with anatomy, and Capella's *L'Anthropologia* (1533), dealing with personal singularities. The contemporary science of anthropology consists of archaeology, cultural anthropology, linguistics, and physical anthropology."

Consensus and arguments are plenty and parallel about the subject matter and sub-divisions. Nevertheless, the broader divisions of anthropology are physical or biological anthropology, and social or cultural, or socio-cultural anthropology. All other divisions either belong to anyone of these two branches or keeping its tie with both the branches.

At present, anthropology is enriched with its various specialisations and methods of study, even though the absolute and isolated study of particular aspect of man's culture and biology will become partial and obverse but not comprehensive. In order to muster the knowledge on man, it requires a blend of sub-divisions in many occasions, since man is a socio-cultural and biological gift of the universe. The interrelationships of different sub-divisions of anthropology are not accidental, but divided for the convenience and also due to the fashions of study of the conglomerate anthropology. Anthropology is a subject, which encompasses man and his environment. Matters that are directly or indirectly related to man are anthropological and according to this perspective, the discipline has diversified and the various specialisations are expanding and updating the science anthropology. This appendix will introduce to you some of the specialisations of anthropology of the present-day.

Biological or Physical Anthropology

Biological or Physical anthropology studies man's biological aspects generally, but the very biological arena put forwards many questions like "what are the peculiarities of man from the other organisms"; "man's position in the animal kingdom"; "the human evolution"; "how long man evolved in the earth and the relationships and semblances of man with other species; and so on. Here, the questions paused before us are not anew, but have long been attempted to answer by many scholars from the onset of the discipline and the efforts for answering are still continuing, and the physical anthropologists are accomplishing the tasks inexhaustibly to comprehend and to update the science of man.

The field of physical anthropology got great impetus from the study of anatomy, and this substantiated much to enhance the study of man's evolution, man's place in the animal kingdom, etc. Besides this, man's anatomical, genotypic (genetic), and phenotypic (physical) characteristics, the peculiarities to possess and create culture and the dialogue between culture and biology within the environment together encompass in physical anthropology.

Some say that physical anthropology is the oldest branch of the discipline—anthropology—and was established much earlier than other branches. Physical anthropology finds time to study man's origin, development and varieties of man, and today there seems to have a shift of emphasis in physical anthropology toward every minute aspect of man.

The subject matter of physical anthropology is quite vast and some of the definitions of it provide a profile of its nexus of research and study. The study of human evolution and human variation are the two principle aspects of physical anthropology. The evolution of modern man through various stages of development and evolutionary process concern physical anthropologists at the first place and the difference in physical characteristics in modern man, including racial differentiation hold the second place. B.M. Das (1997) says, "Physical anthropology is concerned with man as a physical organism in time and space. Here, 'time' means the stages of development of man in the process of evolution during different periods of time, while 'space' refers to the differentiation of physical types in modern man living in different parts of the globe. Thus, physical anthropology has two principal focuses and these are human evolution and human variation."

Apart from this, there are many anthropologists who have delineated the subject matter of physical anthropology and according to Evans Pritchard, physical anthropology is a branch of human biology and comprises such interests as heredity, nutrition, sex differences, the comparative anatomy and physiology of races, and the theory of human evolution. Tylor asserted that, the study of human biology, dealing with racial differences, the development of the human organism, changes in body over the generations, and the relation between ecology and organism. It is also called 'somatology' or 'somatic anthropology'.

Physical anthropology has been diversified into a number of specialisations today and some of the divisions have developed into independent disciplines like genomic studies. At the same time, some of the olden subdivisions become unsophisticated to perform the recent trends in physical anthropology. However, a pertinent overview of the divisions and specialised fields of physical anthropology is given below.

Evolution

Evolution is the process by which different organisms have developed with some modification from earlier existing forms due to change and adaptation. Human evolution is a major concern of physical anthropology. The concept of evolution is used in physical anthropology in tracing the development of Homo sapiens. There are many similarities in the physical structure and functions of lower animals and of man. It was Charles Darwin who presented a systematic arrangement of organisms in the hierarchy of evolution. Man bears the zenith of this hierarchy. According to Darwin, natural selection is the most important process of evolution. "Survival of the fittest" may otherwise said to be natural selection. Apart from this, there are some factors also contributed for human evolution, namely, mutation, genetic drift, migration, isolation, adaptive radiation irreversibility and extinction.

Mutation is the sudden change spontaneously occurring in hereditary material, which thoroughly altering the phenotype of the individual. Mutation is otherwise called as discontinues variations, because it appears without intermediate stages. Mutation results in the emergence of new species. There are various types of mutations, namely, Gene mutation or point mutation, Chromosomal mutation, Biochemical mutation, Genomatic mutation, etc. Genetic drift or "bottle-neck effect" is the change in the genetic composition of a population and it is more effective in small populations. Migration results in the mixing up of genetical composition of different populations. Geographic isolation may restrict the conjugal or reproductive activity, but conjugal isolation is the ultimate thing, which preserves the diversity of population.

There are many theories of evolutions, namely, Lamarck's theory of evolution, Neo-Lamarckism, Darwin's theory of evolution—Theory of natural selection, Theory of artificial selection, Theory of sexual selection, Neo-Darwinism and the Synthetic theory of evolution. Some scholars like Theodosius Dobzhansky confessed that "Biologists have been so preoccupied with providing that man is a product of organic evolution that they have scarcely noticed that man is an extraordinary and unique product of this evolution. He is unique in a purely biological sense. Some forces, which are important in the evolution of man, occur at most as vestiges in the evolution of other creatures. The leading forces of human evolution are intelligence, ability to use linguistic symbols, and the culture, which man has developed. These exclusively, or nearly exclusively, human phenomena affect the biological evolution of man so profoundly that it cannot be understood without taking them into account. Conversely, human society and culture are products of the biological evolution of our species. Human evolution is wholly intelligible only as an outcome of the interaction of biological and social forces. Biologists and sociologists are equally guilty of underestimation of this fact."

The present scene of anthropology necessitates more specialized sub-fields and simultaneously a blend of them is necessary to study every aspect of man and the science of anthropology is strongly need to be reconsidered for man and by man.

Anthropometry

Earlier, anthropometry was the principal concern in the study of race and racial variation. Anthropometry is the measurement of man, his stature, bodily proportions, length and breadth of head, etc. Taking measurement on living body is referred to as Somatometry, and the comparative anatomy of the skull or cranium of man to anthropoid ape, chimpanzee, gorilla, etc., called 'Craniometry'. Oesteometry and Ergonomics are included in anthropometry. Every technological development is indispensably related with man's biological and cultural aspects. For example, a typewriter or a pen or a camera or a pistol or an automobile or any other machine is designed to use it comfortable for man. The keys of a typewriter or the pause trigger of a video camera, etc., are aptly designed because the man-machine relationship has been studied and applied carefully during the production of every machine or tool and the study of man-machine relationship is called as Ergonomics. Oesteometry deals with the measurements of bone other than that of skull.

Nutritional anthropology also has a significant metric method, which provides the study of nutrition and health relations and problems. *Physiometry* is the measurement of human physiology. Human growth and development are also the specific interests of physical anthropology. The colour of skin, hair and eyes, and similar qualitative measures are also taken. Anthroposcopy is the visual examination and reporting of physical traits that cannot be measured exactly, for example eye colour, etc., comes under the study of anthroposcopy. Anthropometry have long been undertaken the study of race and racial variation, the rate of growth of man, and the differences and similarities between different populations. Somatoscopy is also a related area and it is the observation and study of the bodily parts like skin colour, hair colour, eye colour, face form, nose form, lip, etc. In general, all these aspects have helped to classify the races or different populations of the world; therefore, anthropometry contributed to a great extent to the classical physical anthropology and at present the biological anthropologists are engaged in genetic studies instead of anthropometry. It is also identified that "racial purity as a myth", which put a full stop for racial classification.

Human Genetics

Genetics is the science that deals with heredity and variation. Genetic peculiarities and disorders are also comprised under this head. Gregor Johan Mendel (1822-1884) is often called the "father of genetics". This branch of physical anthropology studies man's genesis and human heredity. It studies the genotypic and phenotypic characteristics of man. It was the Danish geneticist Johansen who coined the expressions phenotype and genotype. The physical form and appearances of an organism is called phenotype, and its genic composition is called the genotype. Human genetics, the subfield of physical anthropology, is much developed and there are various allied subdivisions for human genetics, they are namely, Molecular genetics, Health genetics, Genetic engineering, Human biochemical genetics, Human cytogenetics, Human population genetics, Demogenetics or Genetic demography, Developmental genetics, Medical or Clinical genetics, etc.

Dermatoglyphics and Criminal Anthropology

Dermatoglyphics is the study and analysis of the ridge patterns or configurations of the skin of fingers, palms, toes and soles. The dermatoglyphic patterns are stable and permanent traits throughout one's life and this permanency of dermatoglyphic pattern have been used for various purposes. Jan Evangelist Purkinje, the anatomist and experimental physiologist used fingerprints for the identification and classification in 1823. In

1853, Sir William J. Herschel used native handprints as a seal on documents and in 1877; it was the beginning to use fingerprints for official purposes. Even today, the thumbprints are being used instead of signatures and particularly of the illiterate people. The meticulous and particular fingerprints found from the context of a crime, and the investigation and the analysis of the dermatoglyphic patterns of the suspected would help to find out the criminal.

Criminal anthropology is the study of the relationship of various traits and physical characteristics to criminality. Cesare Lombroso (1836–1909) is considered to be the founder of criminal anthropology. Modern studies of crime have established the complex aetiology of criminal behaviour. Physical characteristics like dermatoglyphic pattern as well as psychological and behavioural patterns are also scrutinised to understand the criminal behaviour.

Primatology, Primate Biology, and Primate Behaviour

Primatology is the study of the order primates, usually the non-human primates. It is essential that the study of fossil primates in affiliation to geo-chronological sequence and this would help to understand the evolutionary stages of man. Tyson, in 1699, started the study by describing a Chimpanzee's anatomy. Such studies offer comparative norms that help explain human development. Primatology consists the study of primate biology and primates entail some particular progression. The study of primate biology and primate behaviour is logical to substantiate human evolution and to comprehend the close relationship with the apes and monkeys. B.M. Das has emphasized the relevance of the study of primates through four angles, and he says that, "physical anthropologists are interested in studying the primates, the close relatives of man, from different angles for different reasons. First, the study of fossil primates in relation to geological and temporal sequence. This helps in understanding the evolutionary stages. Second, the comparative anatomical study of the living primates. Anatomical features include bone, morphological features, blood chemistry, dermatoglyphic traits and the like. Third, the study of primate behaviour in their natural surroundings. Fourth, the experimental study of apes and monkeys in the laboratory. This is to understand certain fundamental aspects of man and these animals. Thus primatology is an important aspect of physical anthropology."

Palaeo Anthropology

Palaeo anthropology is the study of the early types of man. It is argued that through the study of fossilised or unfossilised skeletal remains, it could be possible to understand the development of man and this area of study is referred to as human palaeontology. Palaeo anthropology, human palaeontology, primate palaeontology, etc., are inextricably related to each other. Human palaeontology is essentially the study of fossil remains and it helps to trace the evolution of life and culture of man of the past geographical period.

Primate palaeontology is the study of the fossil remains of the order primates, which includes man, the great apes, monkeys, tarsiers and lemurs, to understand man's development and evolution. Of course, all we know that man did not acquire his present phenotypic and genotypic qualities in a day but through ages by a process of gradual development from his non-human ancestors and as it is proved with some excavated fossil remains. Palaeo anthropology is concerned with the study of human societies which lived in the distant past from the time when they were free from animal ancestry until they became modern. Their study is made with the help of artifactual, and non-artifactual remains including the skeletal remains.

Blood Group Studies

A new approach to classify human races based on the blood types has attained a considerable relevance in physical anthropology and the contributions of Landsteiner, Levine, and Wiener are important. The ABO blood group (1900-1902), the MNSs blood group system (1927), and the Rh blood type (1940) have been employed to classify human races of the world.

Serology and Osteology

Serology and osteology are also the important aspects of study in physical anthropology. Serology is the study of blood serum and its constituents. Osteology is the study dealing with an organism's bone structure. Racial anthropology is another area and the study of different types found within the human species and their origins and interrelationships are coming under racial anthropology. The study of interrelations between geographical environment and man is called anthropogeography. Apart from this, Physiological anthropology, Anthropology of twins, Demography, Population structure, Population Variation, and Human growth and development are also the specialised fields coming under physical anthropology.

Applied Physical Anthropology

Every science has theoretical and applied aspects likewise the application of the doctrine of physical anthropology in various fields is becoming pervasive. The application of physical anthropology in the armed service, defence service, forensic, criminal, medical fields, and industrial fields are some of the areas where the applications of physical anthropology are becoming popular.

Recent Physical Anthropology

In physical anthropology too, there have been developed some recent trends during the last six decades and it is mentioned as 'Recent Physical Anthropology' or 'New Physical Anthropology' and the earliest attempts in physical anthropology are referred to as 'Old' or 'Classical Physical Anthropology'. The earliest attempts in physical anthropology were primarily based on the descriptive accounts of the explicit peculiarities of the bodily characteristics like different nose forms, eyes, eye colour, hair types, height, skin colour, etc. But in the recent years, the emphasis has been shifted from traits to populations. That is, the new emphasis is on the influences affecting the biological nature of populations, and the method, in general, is more precise definition of the population under study, and of exact details of its structure: degrees of isolation, size, regional subgroups, age, sex, social, or economic divisions, mating patters, and the whole environmental background (Howells, 1965). Further, Howells argued that this new emphasis in physical anthropology contrasts with earlier work, which often interested in classification, tended to generalise and typologise, blurring important minor distinctions and losing information by doing so. He says, "much of recent work can be called microevolution, investigating small scale differentiation and change in man; it makes much more use of theory and information from genetics and biology, and has more advanced statistical methods for testing and control."

Of course, there were consensus and disagreements on the old and new ideas of physical anthropology. Reddi (1992) differentiates that, "the old or classical physical anthropology which represents the descriptive stage of the subject was mostly characterised by anthropometric studies involving the taking of measurements and classification of indices and computation of statistics. This approach with emphasis on taxonomy remained static till the emergence of the science of genetics and its applications in the interpretation of evolutionary theory. The new physical anthropology on the other hand is mainly interested in understanding the process and mechanisms involved in the problem and classification as such plays a minor part. Here, the theory is critical and the major objective is to develop consistent hypothesis that should be verified experimentally.

According to Reddi (1992), the new physical anthropology started investigation into a number of new areas such as the different blood group systems to understand genetic relationship to trace possible ancestors, and to study the dynamics of the diversity of mankind; biochemical human genetics covering haemoglobins; haptoglobin; transferrins; analysis of evolutionary factors such as mutation, natural selection, genetic drift and gene flow, and primate biology involving the study of blood groups, genetics and local evolutionary factors of non-human primates such as monkeys and apes.

Social and Cultural Anthropology

Social and Cultural Anthropology is considered to be one of the broadest division of anthropology and the other broad division is Physical/Biological anthropology. Socio-cultural anthropology studies man's cultural and social evolution, diffusion, functional and structural aspects, etc. The study of the origin and development of Homo sapiens through the biological point of view is comprised under physical anthropology, but in contrast social and cultural anthropology exert its attention in the study of the origin and development of social and cultural aspects of man. The growing necessity of the minute aspects of study of man became a major force in the bifurcation of the discipline and it results in the stipulation of a number of subdivisions for social and cultural anthropology.

Social Anthropology

Social anthropology and cultural anthropology are the two traditions and often treated as two separate branches of anthropology. Social anthropology deals with societies, and social organisation, family, marriage, kinship, economic organisation, political organisation, religion, law, social process, social system, social structure, social change, etc., of primitive as well as modern and contemporary societies of man have long been some of the areas of interest of social anthropologists.

Some early anthropologists regarded social anthropology as a branch of sociological studies. But the developments in methodology of social anthropology have uplifted it as an independent discipline. Emile Durkheim's thought has been influenced to shape this discipline. Even so, while discussing on the theoretical developments of social anthropology, Evans Pritchard has argued that "Durkheim's importance in the history of the conceptual development of social anthropology in this country [UK] might have been no greater than it has been in America had it not been for the influence of his writings on Professor A.R. Radcliffe-Brown and Prof. B. Malinowski, the two men who have shaped social anthropology into what it is in England today" (Evans-Pritchard, 1950).

There are many other anthropologists also who have contributed to the development of social anthropology and some have attempted to define social anthropology. According to Tylor, social anthropology is "the study of social behaviour, especially from the point of view of the systematic comparative study of social forms and institutions. The aim of social anthropology has been the application of the inductive method to society. The term was originally applied only to the study of the social organisation of non-literate peoples. Social anthropology has largely been a qualitative discipline."

Evans-Pritchard (1950) says that, "social anthropology studies, social behaviour, generally in institutionalised forms, such as the family, kinship systems, political organisation, legal procedures, religious cults, and the like, and the relations between such institutions: and it studies them either in contemporaneous societies or in historical societies for which there is adequate information of the kind to make such studies feasible."

In general, social anthropology has long been kept some particular view other than cultural anthropology and the debates are still persisting about the concepts and methods of social anthropology.

Cultural Anthropology

The study of man as a cultural being, his work, behaviour, social patterns, etc., is the main subjects of study of the cultural anthropologists. "Edward Burnett Tylor is commonly regarded, with justice, as the father of modern cultural anthropology" (Firth, 1973 : 111). The appellation like 'cultural anthropology', 'social anthropology', 'social and cultural anthropology' are being used alternatively by many anthropologists throughout the world. Cultural anthropology is sometimes used almost interchangeably in America for what in England is called social anthropology, reflecting the traditional British interest in social systems and the major interest in culture for American anthropologists. There are some demarcations, however, which have been made by the exponents of both social anthropology and cultural anthropology.

The emphasis of social anthropology is on "societies" and it is "culture" for cultural anthropologists. The term "culture" was adopted by the nineteenth-century anthropologists. Tylor's definition for culture is considered as a "classical definition for the concept of culture." Tylor says that, "culture is that complex whole which includes knowledge, belief, art, morals, law, custom, and any other capabilities and habits acquired by man as a member of society" (Tylor, 1871). There are anthropologists like Ralph L. Beals and Harry Hoijer, Robert Linton, A.L. Kroeber, and others who have defined the term culture. According to Herskovits, culture is the manmade part of the environment. In general, cultural anthropology studies the culture of man synchronically and diachronically, and the subject matter of cultural anthropology is as wider as mankind and culture.

Ethnology is also a term coined for cultural anthropology and ethnology is the study of culture of man on a comparative way. According to Evans-Pritchard, the task of ethnology is to classify peoples on the basis of their racial and cultural characteristics and then to explain their distribution at the present time, or in past times, by the movement and mixture of peoples and the diffusion of cultures (Evans-Pritchard, 1950).

Archaeological Anthropology

The word archaeology comes from the Greek word 'Archaios' meaning ancient or 'Arche' meaning beginning, and 'Logos' meaning study or science. Archaeology is also called as prehistory and it is considered to be a branch of anthropology that adds the dimension of time to the study of culture. Archaeology is related with the historical reconstruction of man and his culture and it helps us to understand the process of cultural change. It reveals the past life of man and his material features, including how people lived and the excavated material culture provides information regarding man's prehistory.

Prehistoric Anthropology or Palaeoanthropology

Prehistoric anthropology studies man's life and culture of the prehistoric times and it is evident that there are no written records about his culture and biology. Hence, this branch is rely on cultural remains of the past, for example tools, artefacts, dwelling place, and the fossil remains of skeletal materials of early man to study and reconstruct his life. According to Evans-Pritchard, Prehistoric archaeology is best regarded as a branch of ethnology. It attempts to reconstruct the history of people and cultures from human and cultural remains found by excavation in geological deposits. It also rely on circumstantial evidence and, like ethnology, can tell social anthropologists little about the ideas and institutions, in which they would be interested, of the peoples whose bones and artefacts it discovers and classifies.

Prehistoric archaeology is the study of those cultures, which did not leave written records. An eminent archaeologist Burkitt is of the opinion that, "prehistory is the subject which deals with the story of man and everything that concerns him from that dim remote moment when he first emerged from his animal ancestry until the time when the existence of written records leads the investigator into the realm of history proper" (Burkitt, 1963).

Archaeology or prehistory deals with ancient cultures and modern civilisation. It attempts to reconstruct the cultural forms of the past and to trace their progress and development. Many archaeological excavations have brought to light a mass of objects which include tools, pots, artefacts, and other weapons, monuments and relics, art and craft of ancient people, human skeletons, etc. The study of these materials provides the story of early man and his culture.

Archaeology is much related to social and cultural anthropology despite it does not mean that it is not related to physical anthropology. Fossilised and semi-fossilised skeletal materials of early man have been excavated and this brought light to man's evolutionary stages. Thus, archaeology is an inextricable element of physical anthropology too.

On the basis of periods or chronological context, the archaeology has been divided into three branches and they are Prehistoric archaeology, Protohistoric archaeology and Historical archaeology. Prehistoric archaeology deals with the study of the past of man before he learned to write and it has been referred to as prehistory or prehistoric archaeology. Historical archaeology deals with the period for which written records are also available. Protohistory is the study of people who were living after history began, but who themselves did not have writing.

Archaeology can also be classified on the basis of the subject matter or the problem of study. Some of the branches are as follows: Economic archaeology, Ethno-archaeology, Under-water archaeology, Aerial archaeology, and Salvage archaeology.

Economic Archaeology paid more attention to the economic motives and compulsions of the past societies. The growth of this branch has been significant in the last twenty-five years, particularly in the field of prehistory.

The study of Ethno-archaeology uses the methods of social and cultural anthropology to understand the comparative anatomy and style of tools and customs of early man and contemporary "primitive" man.

Underwater archaeology or Marine archaeology requires special equipments and skills to go to the deepest of sea to study the wrecks of ancient boats, ships, etc., this would help to understand the technological developments, population migration, trade, war, and the like of the man who belong to the prehistoric and historic times.

Aerial archaeology studies with the help of the aerial photographic techniques. The archaeologist surveys the archaeological sites and prepares maps and plans of the old landmarks and it also provides assumptions of ancient cities.

The archaeologists are often called upon to do something to rescue the archaeological sites or monuments from the destruction that is possible to occur with the advent of construction worked and other developmental works, and this branch is known as salvage archaeology. This involves the transplantation of ancient monuments to a safer place. In recent years, archaeologists have developed sound methods and techniques of survey and excavation work in salvage operations. Some computer software are also have been developed today, and apart from these, an increasing number of private companies are moving into the business of archaeological excavations, since the rush of development projects are outpacing the ability of academic institutions to conduct excavations before beginning various construction projects. There are at least ten such companies functioning in Japan for the last fifteen years, but some academics, however, are concerned about the entry of private companies in archaeological projects.

In essence, archaeology is a discipline reconstructing the total life and culture of ancient man through the study of material culture. The initial material cultures of ancient man was divided by a three ancient system or age system, which was introduced by C.J. Thomson, a Danish prehistorian, in 1836. That was primarily based on the materials by which they had prepared the implements. Accordingly, three divisions such as Stone Age, Bronze Age, and Iron Age were introduced. That was, in fact, the first scientific categorisation of the material cultural evidences. The developments in archaeology are pervasive throughout the world today. The network of archaeological and anthropological interests is also strengthened inextricably.

Ecological Anthropology

The study of man in relationship with the environment, subsumed as ecological anthropology. Ecology is the study of organisms in their largest home—the nature. The study of the interrelationships between organisms and their environment is called 'Ecology' or 'Environmental Biology'. The two basic components of ecological study are organism and environment. But in anthropology, the emphasis is shifted from organism to man, hence ecological anthropology is the study of the relationships between humans and their environment. That is man-environment relations are generally referred to as the subject matter of ecological anthropology and this perspective has been employed by many anthropologists to trace some natural events and social phenomena and also some bio-cultural aspects in relation with physical milieu.

According to James N. Anderson, "ecology comprises all aspects of man as a bio-cultural animal as they are subsumed within the structure and functioning of ecosystems, including human morphology, reproduction, population genetics, stress physiology, nutritional requirements, the ecology of health and disease, and human adaptability. It also encompasses human population ecology—that is, population process: fertility, mortality, migration and population structure—the feedback between biological and cultural factors (technological, economic, organisational) in populations, spatial and economic distribution, and ecological consequences of population trends. Individual biological and population process are interrelated with ecological perceptions, environmental cognition, language as cultural codification, ideology, creative thinking, planning, and decision-making. Finally, this holistic conception of ecology includes the adaptiveness and non-adaptiveness of human behaviour and institutions viewed in their widest context. It poses the questions of the degree to which technological, economic, social, political, ritual, aesthetic, and ideological organisations are adaptive and maladaptive; whether the feed-back of human behaviour and institutions on the earth's ecosystems is positive or negative, and to what degree; and whether ethics, purposive policy, and planning are ecologically beneficial or detrimental. It is concerned with problems of urban-industrial ecosystems, environmental aesthetics, design and planning, government-citizen interactions, and environmental law and policy-making."

The environment, culture and the ecological perspectives are being used by many cultural anthropologists to explain why particular traits or aggregations of traits exist at particular times and in particular places; and how the traits or congeries of traits function or behave at particular times and particular places. The explanations to these questions are of general interests to cultural anthropologists, and there are some approaches and perspectives employed in this direction are the environmental determinism, environmental possibilism, the ecological perspective, cultural ecology, population ecology, systems ecology, and ethnoecology.

Environmental determinism and possibilism are the two views on environmental influences distinguished during the first two decades of the 20th Century. The environmental determinism is also referred to as 'determinism' or 'environmentalism'. The exponents of environmental determinism argued that environmental forms ordain culture. That is, in this view, culture is viewed as passive and environment as an active force moulding culture to its pattern.

This view holds that cultures act selectively upon their environments and exploiting some possibilities while ignoring others. That is environment is passive and the culture take an active role in shaping culture. This view is often referred to as possibilism and which is a reverse concept of environmental determinism.

The ecological perspective is more comprehensive. The environmental determinism and possibilism examines two opposing views. The environmental determinism holds the idea that the environment is active in shaping culture, whereas the possiblism emphasise on culture, which is active, and the environment is passive. Both of these concepts considered to be insufficient hence one aspect cannot be understood without considering the other, and this postulation renders the theoretical foundation of ecology; and this is the third major theme in environmental thought. The ecological perspective provides a more precise understanding of the relationship between man and environment.

The doctrine Cultural Ecology, one of the turning points in ecological anthropology, was developed under the leadership of the American anthropologist Julian Steward during 1940–1960. Steward was interested not merely in establishing environmental-cultural relationships but also developing a theoretical and methodological scheme for understanding development of human societies. Three fundamental procedures of cultural ecology are set forth by Steward and they are: (1) the analysis of the relation between environment and exploitative or productive technology; (2) the behaviour patterns involved in the exploitation of a particular area by means of particular technology; and (3) the extent to which the behaviour patterns entailed in exploiting the environment affect other aspects of culture."

Population ecology is the study of those processes that affect the distribution and abundance of ecological populations. The ecological population is a local group of organisms, belonging to the same species with a distinctive lifestyle. The study of particular human groups and their environmental relations was actually introduced by Julian Steward's cultural ecology and this juncture is considered to be the beginning of population.

Systems Ecology is also an important aspect. The studies in ecological anthropology through a new perspective based upon the concept of the system can be referred to as systems ecology. The system focuses upon a complex network of mutual causality. The methods of systems analysis are used to define the boundaries and environments of a system and also to model its complexity in such a way that system behaviour can be studied.

To study ecological relationships from the participant's point of view is referred to as ethnoecology and it is also called as ethnoscience, ethnographic semantics, or cognitive ethnography. According to James N. Anderson, the first aim of ethnoecologist is to describe what people know about nature and second to describe how people use this knowledge to get along in the world. Ethnoecology uses the concepts of structural linguistics and the investigations are being advocated by some anthropologists with training in linguistics. Ethnoecologists depend chiefly upon verbal eliciting techniques to tap classifications of the structure of specific analytically separate cognitive spheres. The prefix 'ethno' is referring to a people's own view or knowledge of some subject matter. "The aim of the ethnological approach is simply to present a people's view of behaviour appropriate to that setting" (Rappaport and Vaida, 1968).

Forensic Anthropology

Forensic anthropology is a subdiscipline of biological or physical anthropology and this division carry out research, study and analysis on forensic aspects. Forensic anthropology has progressed to a formally recognised subdiscipline today and a multidisciplinary approach is employed in it to resolve medico-legal cases. Physical anthropologists, pathologists, dentists and experts in serology, dermatogliphics and hair analysis are employed in finding out medico-legal cases.

Clyde Collins Snow (1982), an American consultant in forensic anthropology, has defined forensic anthropology as "the application of the physical anthropologist's specialised knowledge of human sexual, racial, age, and individual variation to problems of medical jurisprudence." Snow points out that T.D. Stewart's (1979) definition of forensic anthropology is not broader since it restricts the scope of forensic anthropology to the identification of human skeletal remains. Further, Snow has demarcated the field of forensic anthropology and according to which, although as presently practiced forensic anthropology is largely concerned with skeletal identification, there are other, non-osteological facts of human biological variation falling within the purview of physical anthropology that are of medico-legal importance.

Thomas Dwight (1843–1911) is considered as "the Father of Forensic Anthropology" in the United States. But, George Dorsey was the first anthropologist to serve as a forensic expert in the United States. Today, forensic anthropology has well progressed in the United States.

Economic Anthropology

Communication between anthropologists and economists is steadily increasing, especially since anthropologists have become aware of the need to record as fully as possible the economic mechanisms of the societies they study (Herskovits, 1955 : 5).

Man has unlimited wants, but resources to satisfy wants are limited. This creates diverse problems in different societies. The availability, spread, and use of food, shelter, and clothing; and the goods, technology, services, etc., varies in different cultural milieu. This has resulted in a number of problems, but most of the problems essentially pertains to wants. In order to resolve the problems, man himself has separated and makes conspicuous the rules involved in human needs and it became economics; whereas the study of man's economic problems through the anthropological view is referred to as economic anthropology.

Most early anthropologists studied and depicted the economic aspects of life of the "primitive" people and also many tribal communities. In fact, in those period anthropologists studied mostly on tribal studies and the study of "primitive man", but along with the developments in the discipline anthropology, it started studying every problem of man in the world. As a result of which some of the early connotations of economic anthropology have been discarded by many scholars and it began to possess a comprehensive nature towards the economic anthropological aspects of mankind.

According to Ralph L. Beals (1982), "the most important aspect of economics is its place in the total social system. Beals emphasised on problems of production, distribution, and consumption of goods and the role of an extensive and elaborate exchange system with aboriginal antecedents. In my personal view, economic anthropology can be defined as a subdiscipline of anthropology which studies the modes of compensation involved in most human interactions and its rules in every society, in par with man's bio-cultural existence."

Political Anthropology

This branch includes the study of the nature, meaning and functioning of various political institutions and governmental forms in human groups everywhere. Etymologically, the word politics is derived from the Greek word "Polis" meaning city and it was the state of ancient Greek. The study of the activities of the 'Polis' was called politics. Political anthropology encompasses on the whole political aspects of man.

The nature and organisation of every culture and society determines the political characteristics and the study of these characteristics through the anthropological perspective gives an in-depth understanding of every political system since anthropological perspective rely on the socio-cultural and biological matters of man.

Makhan Jha (1994) says "the traditional tribal panchayat or the modern elected body, the organisation of their government, tribal law and justices, etc. are briefly the subject of the political anthropology." Balandier (1972 : 3) envisaged "political anthropology as a [sub]discipline concerned with 'archaic' societies in which the state is not clearly constituted and societies in which the state exists and takes on a wide variety of forms."

Political system is not static one anywhere in the world. It changes from time to time. Socio-cultural factors and the politics itself are the basis of this non-static or dynamic nature. Among several tribal or aboriginal people their traditional political institutions and systems are prevalent without much changes, whereas many people lost their traditional system basically due to the "powerful political system" of different countries. The invasion of the political system of the mainstream to tribes and aboriginal people has obviously been devastated the traditional system in many regions of the world. The interests of most early anthropologists were on the political organisation of the tribes and "primitive people", but the changing situation has been strongly emphasised on the study of the complete nuances of political systems of all societies in the world.

Applied Anthropology

In India, during the colonial period, the British administrators realised that a good awareness of the natives would be a pre-requisite to rule the people properly. With this forethought, the British have made voluminous works on the culture and society of the heterogeneous population of India.

The study of every ethnic group becomes an indispensable aspect while planning and implementing programmes for the development of the people of India. These early efforts are the underpinning of anthropology and particularly applied anthropology in India. The works of Risley (1891), Dalton (1972), Edgar Thurston (1909), Radcliffe Brown (1922), Hutton (1931), Rivers (1906), and others are a few to mention in this regard.

Applied anthropologists need an especially high degree of consciousness of what is and is not possible, of what has historically been possible and what has not; optimism—yes—but also realism, and a stronger sense of scepticism, too. They will also need an exceptionally thick skin" (Ralph Grillo, 1998 : 31). He (*ibid.*, 3) opined, "Anthropology has much to offer the world of development—though that world has yet to be completely convinced of its value. But we must be fully aware of what involvement in that world means, ethically, politically and practically."

L.P. Vidyarthi (1968) has had delineated the major realms of the applied anthrcpology in his book 'Applied Anthropology in India'. According to it: (1) Education and culture, (2) Health and culture, (3) Family planning, (4) Applied Physical Anthropology studies, (5) Studies of Crime and Criminal Communities, (6) Industrial and Urban Planning, (7) Agriculture Extensions, (8) Labour Research, (9) Need of Leadership studies in Applied Anthropology, (10) Studies of Military organisation, and (11) Community Development are some of the major areas of applied anthropology.

The term 'Applied Anthropology' is not of recent origins. It was used by D.G. Brinton in his speech as early as 1875, but it came into use before the late 1920s and middle 1930 (Vidyarthi, 1968). According to Firth and Hogbin (1957), the phrase 'applied anthropology' was first used in print by Radcliffe-Brown (1931). In the words of Foster, "applied anthropology refers to the professional activities of anthropologists in programmes which have as primary goals changes in human behaviour believed to ameliorate contemporary social, economic and technological problems, rather than the development of social and cultural theory" (Foster, 1969 : 54; quoted in Grillo, 1998). The Indian anthropologist, Makhan Jha (1994 : 12) says, "in the broadest sense, this term [applied anthropology] refers to the use of anthropological concepts, methods, theories and findings for a specific purpose of solving the problems which confront the societies." Whereas the American anthropologist, Ralph L. Beals (1982 : 21) opined that applied anthropologists are really a quasi-professional groups. They are not specialisations of the discipline but rather represent extensions in its application.

During the colonial period, Malinowski had published a paper on 'practical anthropology' in 1929, and it gained much attention. But the use of the phrase 'practical anthropology' for the present 'applied anthropology' did not received an acceptance among scholars today. Despite, Grillo (1998) has rightly stated the four kinds of activities of the then [that is 1930s] referred and discussed areas of practical or applied anthropology, they are as follows:

1. Research on contemporary society, especially on 'culture contact', later to be called social change, in the colonies;
2. Research into a number of specific problems of concern to colonial administration (not always or even usually at their request);
3. Provision of information and/or advice to those administration; and
4. The involvement of anthropologists in the training of administrators. The application of anthropological knowledge to meet the needs of the group for which the anthropologist is working. This may include giving advice, administration, or giving instruction.

Synthetic Anthropology

Synthetic anthropology has been developed in the last few decades, and it is an approach, which tries to integrate physical anthropology, archaeology, linguistics, theoretical anthropology, and the other cultural and historical sciences.

Cognitive Anthropology

Cognitive anthropology is a new version of cultural anthropology and it emerged during 1955 and 1965. Cognitive anthropologists have made significant steps in the study of semantic organization and formal analysis. Formal analysis, actually, derived with the works of Levi-Strauss, Radcliffe-Brown, Nadel and others. Psycholinguistics and sociolinguistics are allied subjects of cognitive anthropology. Earlier, anthropology was characterised by the method of collection of a pre-existing order of culture and society. Then, the anthropologists were interested to make mere descriptions of material traits and institutions such as house types, family types, kinship types, economic types, personality types, etc. The cognitive anthropologists eschewed from this activity and they are interested in the formal analysis of these aspects. For them cultures are not mere material phenomena but they are cognitive organizations of material phenomena and therefore the exponents of cognitive anthropology attempts to discover the order underlying it. Accordingly, cognitive anthropology endeavours to innform methods for discovering and describing the principles of organization.

Cognitive anthropology studies cultural knowledge, knowledge which is embedded in words, in stories, and artefacts, and which is learned from and shared with other humans. Another notion regarding cognitive anthropology is to study the way in which knowledge is conventionalised into culture. Stephen A. Tyler (1969) argued that "cognitive anthropology is based on the assumption that its data are mental phenomena which can be analysed by formal methods similar to those of mathematics and logic, but traditional cultural anthropology is based on the assumption that its data are discrete material phenomena which can be analysed like the material phenomena of any other natural science."

Symbolic Anthropology

According to Raymond Firth (1973 : 1) "symbolization is a universal human process. But we still need to understand much more about it, especially in its comparative aspects, in different societies, different classes, [and] different religions. Pervasive in communication, grounded in the very use of language, symbolization is part of the living stuff of social relationships." For symbolic anthropologists, the main aim of anthropology is to elucidate the meanings within which humans live and behave.

Symbolic anthropology views culture as a symbolic system that arises basically from human interpretations of the world. Its approach is not cultural materialist. Cultural materialism holds that economic or material factors can explain most of the cultural phenomena of societies. The important aspect of symbolic anthropology is the role of symbols in constructing public meaning and it focuses on how symbols shape our experience as well as how symbols are manipulated by people in social situations.

Philosophical Anthropology

The branch of philosophy is concerned with the essence and distinctive character of man and the place, which he occupies in the universe.

Theological Anthropology

The study of man's nature and characteristics, from the point of view of systematic anthropology. Such subjects as man's creation and the relation between soul and body are considered. The usage is largely continental.

Urgent Anthropology

Urgent anthropology is devoted to rescuing and preserving for the future the wide variety of cultural forms modifying or disappearing rapidly with the impact of the industrial age (Beals, 1982 : 3).

Psychological Anthropology

The study of the relationship between child rearing and personality in different culture forms are the core of psychological anthropology, once known as the field of "culture personality" pioneered by people such as Margaret Mead in anthropology and Abram Kardiner in psychiatry. Psychological anthropology seeks to understand the impact of culture up on the emotional and cognitive development of the individual and to delineate clusters of personality traits characteristic of certain cultures.

The field of psychological anthropology is further concerned with studying the cultural symbols and institutions through which peoples cope with fear, anxiety, and repressed desires.

People derive a sense of release, security, and control through the supernatural personification of the subjects of their buried concerns, but uncovering these processes requires interdisciplinary research. The joint efforts of anthropologists and psychiatrists have thus benefited both disciplines. Psychoanalysis has contributed a theory of socialisation and symbolism to anthropology and anthropology in turn has impressed upon psychoanalytic theory.

Conclusions

Appendix-II is provided for the beginners to have a general understanding on various dimensions of anthropology, which is inevitable for a student of 'Visual Anthropology' and 'Audio-

Visual Anthropology'. As anthropology is an eclectic subject, it has accepted many things from science and technology, language, art, religion, law, history, philosophy, politics, economics, commerce, etc. Anthropological knowledge also provides many things like its methodology, theory, views, etc., to various subjects and disciplines. However, at present, new versions are coming up ceaselessly and some divisions have become not popular and worthless, whereas novel streams of thoughts are coming up today. Dynamic nature is universal, for every culture, society, economy, and technology, etc., and it is a fact that the pace of change varies from one cultural milieu to another. Anthropologists can extend their knowledge towards all spheres of problems of man's life in the world, and the various specialisations are capable of undertaking the tasks ahead and to ameliorate the things better.

Bibliography

Ahuja, B.N. and Chhabra, S.S. 1989. *Communications*. New Delhi: Surjeet Publications.

Andreyeva, Galina, 1980. *Social Psychology*. Moscow: Progress Publishers.

Arnheim, Rudolf, 1958 (1992 rpt). *Film as Art*. Delhi: Rupa & Co.

Balandier, Georges, 1972. *Political Anthropology*. Great Britain: Penguin Books.

Ballon, Rachel, 2005. *Blueprint for Screenwriting—A Complete Writer's Guide to Story Structure and Character Development*. New Jersey: Lawrence Erlbaum Associates Publishers.

Behura, N.K. 1996. Planned Development and Quality of life among Indian Tribes (in) Mann, R.S. (Ed.) *Tribes of India: Ongoing Challenges*. New Delhi: M.D. Publications Pvt. Ltd.

Bhowmick, P. K. 1980. Regional Strategy for the Development of the Tribal Communities (in) Mohapatra and Panda (Eds.) *Tribal Problems of Today and Tomorrow*. Bhubaneswar: Babari Cultural Society and The Modern Book Depot.

Bock, Philip K. 1969. *Modern Cultural Anthropology: An Introduction*. New York: Alfred A. Knopf, Inc.

Brigard, Emilie De, 1975. The History of Ethnographic Film (in) Paul Hockings (Ed.) *Principles of Visual Anthropology*. Paris: Mouton Publishers.

Burkitt, M.C. 1963. *The Old Stone Age: A Study of Palaeolithic Times*. Culcutta: Rupa & Co.

Casey, Bernadette; Neil Casey, Ben Calvert, Liam French and Justin

Lewis, 2004. *Key Concepts in Television Studies*. London: Routledge.

Chakrabarti, S.B. 1987. International Seminar on Visual Anthropology (in) *Human Science* Vol. 36. No. 4. Anthropological Survey of India.

Chakraborty, Jyotirmoy, 1989. Photography as a tool for improved Ethnography (in) *Human Science*. Vol. 38. No. 4. Journal of the Anthropological Survey of India.

Clark, D.S. 1987. *Principles of Semiotics*. New York: Routledge & Kegan Paul.

Crapo, Richley H. 2002. *Cultural Anthropology—Understanding Ourselves and Others*. New York: McGraw-Hill.

Das, B.M. 1997. *Outlines of Physical Anthropology*. Allahabad: Kitab Mahal.

Das, N.K. 1996. The Shifting Cultivation of North East: Problem and Prospectus of Development (in) Mann, R.S. (Ed.) *Tribes of India, Ongoing Challenges*. New Delhi: M.D. Publications Pvt. Ltd.

Deogaonkar, S.G. 1990. *Tribal Exploitation: A Study of Victims of Crime and Bondedness*. New Delhi. Inter-India Publication.

Dougall, David Mac, 1993 rpt. (in) Bill Nichols (Ed.) *Movies and Methods*. Vol. I. Calcutta: Seagull Books.

Ember, Carol R. and Ember, Melvin, 1988. *Anthropology*. New Jersey: Prentice Hall.

Firth, Raymond. 1973. *Symbols: Public and Private*. London: George Allen & Unwin Ltd.

Grillo, Ralph. 1998. *Social Anthropology and Development Policy*. New Delhi: AITBS.

Harries—Jones, Peter, 1998. (in) Bouissac, Paul (Ed.) *Encyclopaedia of Semiotics*. New York: Oxford University Press.

Hartley, John, 2004. *Key Concepts in Communication, Cultural and Media Studies*. London: Routledge.

Hawkes, Terence, 2003. *Structuralism and Semiotics*. London: Routledge.

Hayward, Susan, 2004. *Key Concepts in Cinema Studies*. London: Routledge.

Herskovits, Melville J. 1955. *Cultural Anthropology*. New Delhi: Oxford and IBH Publishing Co.

Hockings, Paul, (Ed.) 1975. *Principles of Visual Anthropology*. The Hague: Mouton Publishers.

Huda, Anwar, 2004. *The Art and Science of Cinema*. New Delhi: Atlantic Publishers and Distributors.

Jakobson, Roman, 1978. *Six Lectures on Sound and Meaning*. Cambridge: The MIT Press.

Jha, Makhan, 1995. *An Introduction to Social Anthropology*. New Delhi: Vikas Publishing House Pvt. Ltd.

Kapoor, A.K. 1996. Tribe, Anthropologist and Future (in) Mann R.S. (Ed.) *Tribes of India: Ongoing Challenges*. New Delhi. M.D. Publications Pvt. Ltd.

Keesing, Roger M. 1981. *Cultural Anthropology: A Contemporary Perspective*. New York: Holt Rinehart and Winston.

Khubchandani, Lachman M. 1992. *Tribal Identity: A Language and Communication Perspective*. Shimla: Indian Institute of advanced Study.

Lal, R.B. and Solanki S.S. 1976. Problems of Tribals in the Hilly Tracts of Gujarat (in) Ranjit Gupta (Ed.), *Planning for Tribal Development*. New Delhi: Ankur Publishing House.

Lehman, Peter (Ed.) 1997. *Defining Cinema*. London: The Athlone Press.

Levi-Strauss, Claude. 1963. (1986 rpt.) *Structural Anthropology*. England: Penguin Books.

Loizos, Peter, 1993. Encountering Ethnographic Films (in) *American Anthropologists*. Chicago: University of Chicago Press.

Mahanti, Neeti, 1994. *Tribal Issues, A non-conventional approach*. New Delhi: Inter-India Publications.

Mahendrakumar, M.S. 1997. Kudayum Thudiyum—Ritual Art (in) *Kerala Calling*. (June 1997) Thiruvananthapuram: Govt. of Kerala.

Mahendrakumar, M.S. 2001. Significance of Ethnographic Filming in the Study of Changing Cultures and Languages (in) *Man and Life*. Vol. 27. Nos. 1 and 2. January-June.

Mahendrakumar, M.S. 2006. *Pecuniarisation—A New Theory of Social Change in India*. New Delhi: Serials Publications.

Mahendrakumar, M.S. 2007. Audio-Visual Anthropology and Its

Application: A Conceptualisation. (in) *Review Projector (India)*, Vol. 10, No. 1. January-March. Quarterly.

Mahendrakumar, M.S. 2012. *Social Change Among the Cultivators*. New Delhi: Discovery Publishing House.

Mann, Gurmeet Singh, 1987. *The Story of Mass Communication: An Indian Perspective*. New Delhi: Harnam Publications.

Mann, R.S. 1980. Problems of Indian Tribes: A Brief Review (in) Vyas, N.N. and Mann, R.S. (Eds.) *Indian Tribes in Transition*. Jaipur: Rawat Publications.

Mathur, P.R.G. *Tribal Situation in Kerala*. Trivandrum: Kerala Historical Society.

Mead, Margaret, 1975. Visual Anthropology in a Discipline of Words (in) Paul Hockings (Ed.) *Principles of Visual Anthropology*. Paris: Mouton Publishers.

Mehta, Shalina, 1996. Tribal Situation in India: Encounters with Empiricism (in) Mann R.S. (Ed.) *Tribes of India: Ongoing Challenges*. New Delhi: M.D. Publications Pvt. Ltd.

Milner, Andrew and Jeff Browitt, 2003. *Contemporary Cultural Theory*. Jaipur: Rawat Publications.

Monaco, James, 2000. *How to Read a Film*. New York: Oxford University Press.

Murphy, Robert F. 1989. *Cultural and Social Anthropology—An Overture*. New Jersey: Prentice Hall.

Nichols, Bill, 1993. *Movies and Methods*. Vol. 1. Calcutta: Seagull Books.

Patel, M.L. 1984. *Planning Strategy for Tribal Development*. New Delhi. Inter-India Publications.

Pattanayak, D.P. 1976. Language and Tribal Planning (in) Ranjit Gupta (Ed.), *Planning for Tribal Development*. New Delhi: Ankur Publishing house.

Pelto, Pertti J. and Pelto, Gretel H. 1970 (1978 rpt.) *Anthropological Research: The Structure of Inquiry*. London: Cambridge University Press.

Pike, Kenneth L. 1993. *Talk, Thought and Thing: The emic road toward conscious knowledge*. Texas: International Academic Bookstore.

Robinson, Andrew, 1995. *The Story of Writing*. London: Thames and Hudson Ltd.

Roy, Rakhi and Jaysinhji Jhala, 1992. *An Examination of the Need and Potential for Visual Anthropology in the Indian Social Context* (in) Singh, K.S. (Ed.) 1992. Visual Anthropology and India. Calcutta: Anthropological Survey of India.

Ruby, Jay, 1996. Visual Anthropology. (in) *Encyclopedia of Cultural Anthropology*, David Levinson and Melvin Ember (Eds.). New York: Henry Holt and Company, Vol. 4: 1345-1351.

Sahay, K.N. 1993. *Visual Anthropology in India and its Development*. New Delhi: Gyan Publishing House.

Scupin, Raymond, 1995. *Cultural Anthropology: A Global Perspective*. New Jersey: Prentice Hall.

Shirley Weitz, 1979. *Non-verbal Communication*. New York: Oxford University Press.

Singh, K.S. (Ed.) 1992. *Visual Anthropology and India*. Calcutta: Anthropological Survey of India.

Smith, Ken; Sandra Moriarty, Gretchen Barbatsis, Keith Kenney (Eds.) 2005. *Handbook of Visual Communication—Theory, Methods, and Media*. New Jersey: Lawrence Erlbaum Associates Publishers.

Sudarsen, V. and Xavier Raj, A. 1996. Tribal Scenario and Developmental Planning in Tamil Nadu (in) Mann R.S. (Ed.) *Tribes of India: Ongoing Challenges*. New Delhi: M.D. Publications Pvt. Ltd.

Tapscott, Don, 1995. *The Digital Economy: Promise and Peril in the Age of Networked Intelligence*. New York: Mc Graw-Hill.

Thwaites, Tony; Lloyed Davis, Warwick Mules, 2005. *Introducing Cultural and Media Studies—A Semiotic Approach*. New York: Palgrave.

Tylor, Edward B. 1988, rpt. *Dictionary of Anthropology*. Delhi: Goyal SaaB Publishers and Distributers.

Tylor, Edward B. 1871 (1929 rpt.) *Primitive Culture—Researches into the Development of Mythology, Philosophy, Religion, Language, Art, and Custom*. Vol. I. London: John Murray.

Venkatesan, D. 1996. Social Mobility through reservation, education and employment among the Scheduled Tribes in India (in) Mann, R.S. (Ed.) *Tribes of India: Ongoing Challenges*. New Delhi: M.D. Publications Pvt. Ltd.

Verma, R.C. 1995. *Indian Tribes through Ages*. New Delhi: Publications Division, Govt. of India.

Vyas, N.N. 1980. *Kadana Resettlement: A case of Tribal Displacement in Southern Rajastan* (in) Vyas, N.N. and Mann, R.S. (Eds.) Indian Tribes in Transition. Jaipur: Rawat Publications.

Vidyarthi, L.P. 1978. *Rise of Anthropology in India*. Vol. II. New Delhi: Concept Publishing Company.

Wolverton, Mike, 1987. *Reality on Reels—How to Make Documentaries for Video/Radio/Film*. Delhi: Surjeet Publications.

Woodiwiss, Anthony, 2001. *The Visual in Social Theory*. London: The Athlone Press.

Wtaker, W. Richard, Janet E. Ramsey, Roland D. Smith, 2004. *Media Writing—Print, Broadcast and Public Relations*. New Jersey: Lawrence Erlbaum Associates Publishers.

Index